HAL LEONARD UKULELE METHOD

Supplement to Any Ukulele Method

EASY SONGS FOR UKULELE

Play the Melodies of 20 Pop, Folk, Country, and Blues Songs

BY LIL' REV

ISBN 978-1-4234-0277-0

7777 W. BLUEMOUND RD. P.O. BOX 13819 MILWAUKEE, WI 53213

For all works contained herein:
Unauthorized copying, arranging, adapting, recording or public performance is an infringement of copyright.
Infringers are liable under the law.

Visit Hal Leonard Online at
www.halleonard.com

INTRODUCTION

Welcome to *Easy Songs for Ukulele*, a collection of 20 pop, folk, country, and blues favorites arranged for easy ukulele. If you're a beginning ukulele player, you've come to the right place; these well-known songs will have you playing, reading, and enjoying music in no time!

This collection can be used on its own or as a supplement to the *Hal Leonard Ukulele Method – Book One* or any other beginning ukulele method. The songs are arranged in order of difficulty. Each melody is presented in an easy-to-read format—including lyrics to help you follow along and ukulele chord diagrams for optional accompaniment. As you progress through the book, you can go back and try playing the chords as well. Additional lyrics are also provided at the end of many of the songs in case you want to sing extra verses.

SONG STRUCTURE

The songs in this book have different sections, which may or may not include the following:

Intro
This is usually a short instrumental section that "introduces" the song at the beginning.

Verse
This is one of the main sections of a song and conveys most of the storyline. A song usually has several verses, all with the same music but each with different lyrics.

Chorus
This is often the most memorable section of a song. Unlike the verse, the chorus usually has the same lyrics every time it repeats.

Bridge
This section is a break from the rest of the song, often having a very different chord progression and feel.

Solo
This is an instrumental section, often played over the verse or chorus structure.

Outro
Similar to an intro, this section brings the song to an end.

ENDINGS & REPEATS

Many of the songs have some new symbols that you must understand before playing. Each of these represents a different type of ending.

1st and 2nd Endings
These are indicated by brackets and numbers. The first time through a song section, play the first ending and then repeat. The second time through, skip the first ending, and play through the second ending.

D.S.
This means "Dal Segno" or "from the sign." When you see this abbreviation above the staff, find the sign (𝄋) earlier in the song and resume playing from that point.

al Coda
This means "to the Coda," a concluding section in the song. If you see the words "D.S. al Coda," return to the sign (𝄋) earlier in the song and play until you see the words "To Coda," then skip to the Coda at the end of the song, indicated by the symbol: ⊕.

al Fine
This means "to the end." If you see the words "D.S. al Fine," return to the sign (𝄋) earlier in the song and play until you see the word "Fine."

D.C.
This means "Da Capo" or "from the head." When you see this abbreviation above the staff, return to the beginning (or "head") of the song and resume playing

CONTENTS

SONG	RECORDING ARTIST	PAGE
Love Me Tender	Elvis Presley	6
All My Loving	The Beatles	8
Goodnight, Irene	Huddie Ledbetter	10
Last Night I Had the Strangest Dream	Simon & Garfunkel	12
Pastures of Plenty	Woody Guthrie	14
I Walk the Line	Johnny Cash	16
The House of the Rising Sun	The Animals	18
This Land Is Your Land	Woody Guthrie	20
I'm So Lonesome I Could Cry	Hank Williams	22
We Shall Overcome	Pete Seeger	25
Your Cheatin' Heart	Hank Williams	27
Nowhere Man	The Beatles	30
Ob-La-Di, Ob-La-Da	The Beatles	32
Heart and Soul	Hoagy Carmichael	34
Blue Eyes Crying in the Rain	Elvis Presley	36
Blue Skies	Irving Berlin	39
Eight Days a Week	The Beatles	42
Tom Dooley	The Kingston Trio	44
Blues Stay Away from Me	The Delmore Brothers	45
Yesterday	The Beatles	46

LOVE ME TENDER

Words and Music by
ELVIS PRESLEY and VERA MATSON

Copyright © 1956; Renewed 1984 Elvis Presley Music (BMI)
Worldwide Rights for Elvis Presley Music Administered by Cherry River Music Co.
International Copyright Secured All Rights Reserved

Additional Lyrics

3. Love me tender, love me dear;
Tell me you are mine.
I'll be yours through all the years,
Till the end of time.

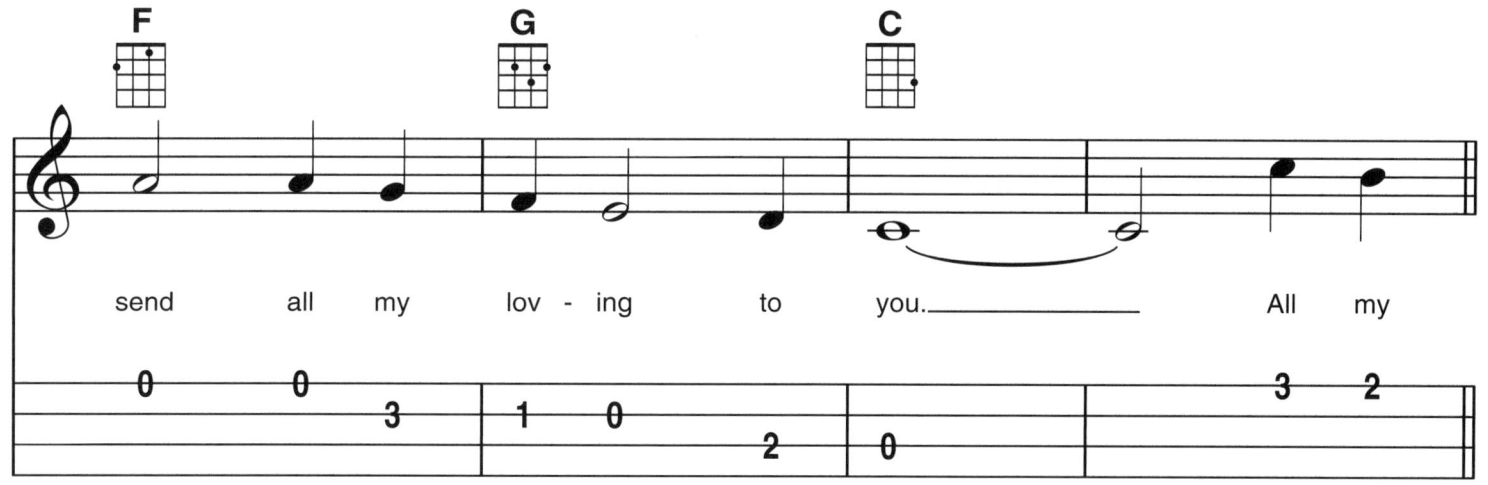

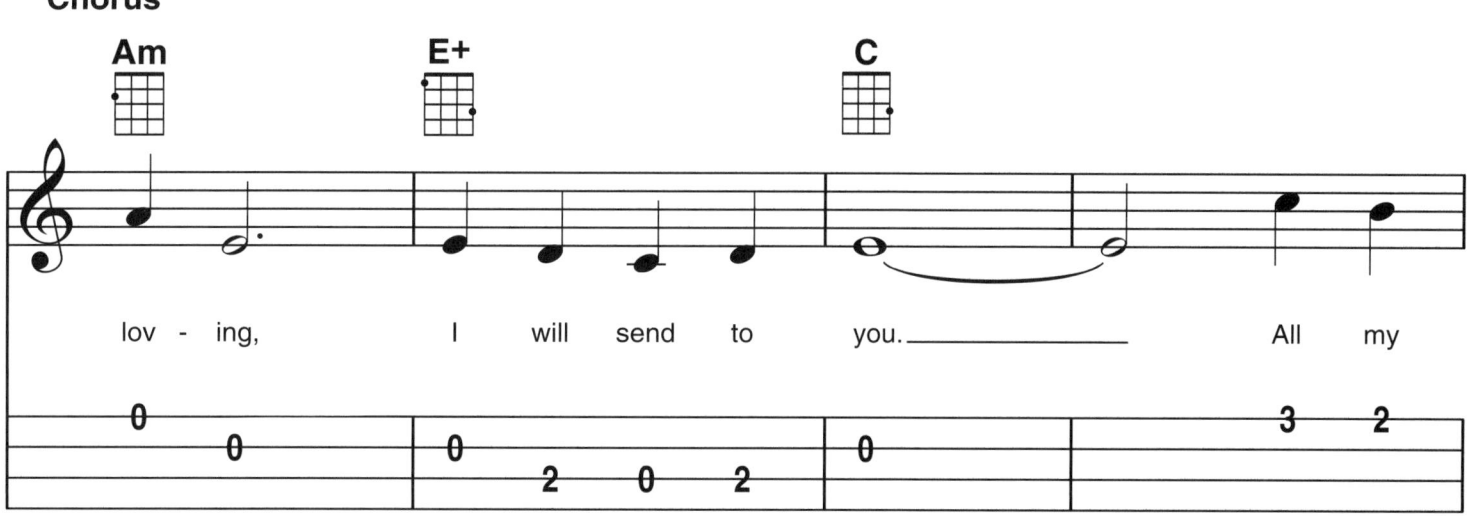

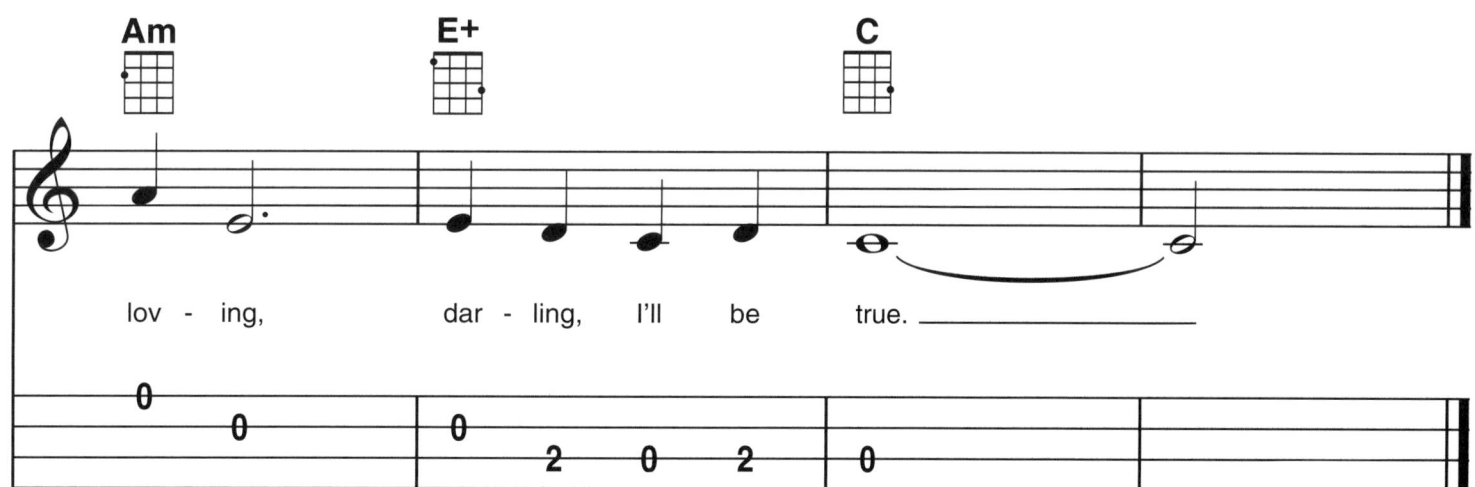

Additional Lyrics

2. I'll pretend that I'm kissing the lips I am missing,
   And hope that my dreams will come true.
   And then while I'm away, I'll write home ev'ry day,
   And I'll send all my loving to you.

Goodnight, Irene

Words and Music by
HUDDIE LEDBETTER and JOHN A. LOMAX

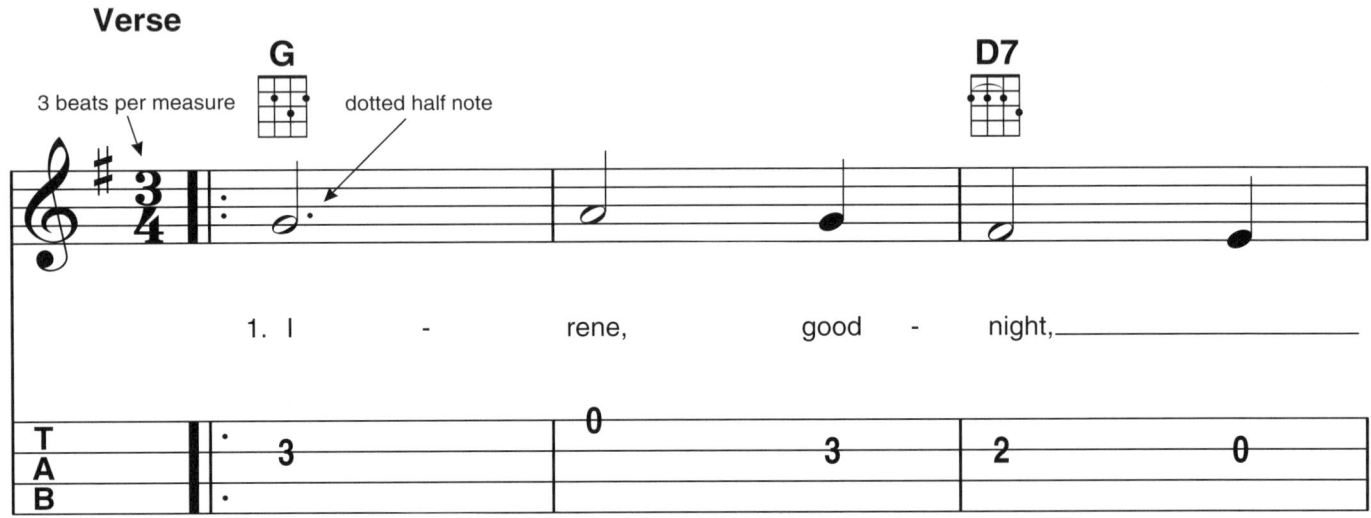

TRO - © Copyright 1936 (Renewed) and 1950 (Renewed) Ludlow Music, Inc., New York, NY
International Copyright Secured
All Rights Reserved Including Public Performance For Profit
Used by Permission

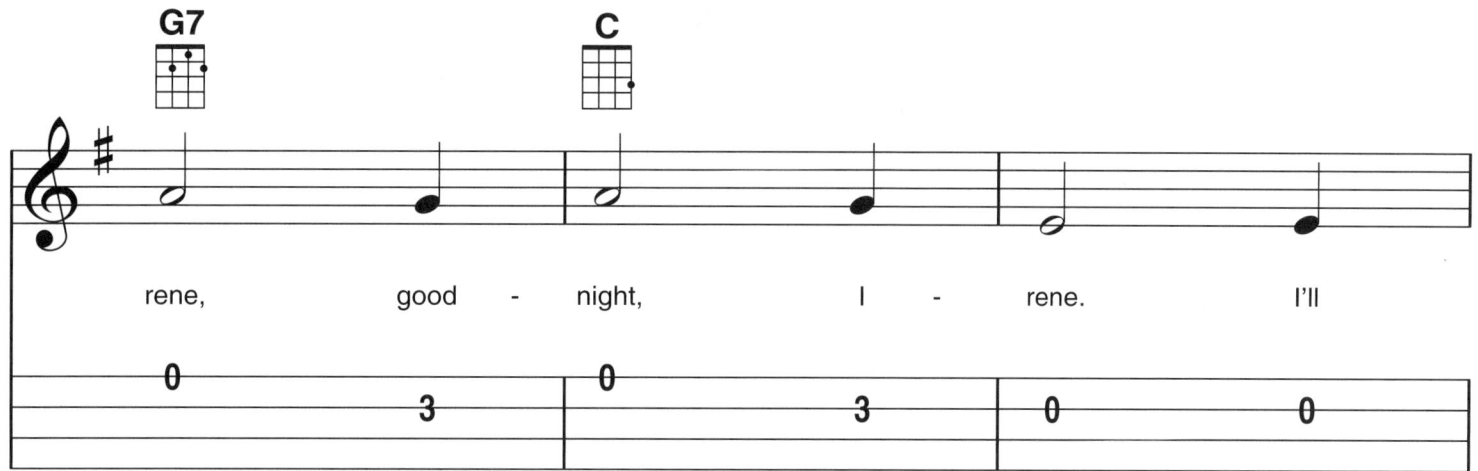
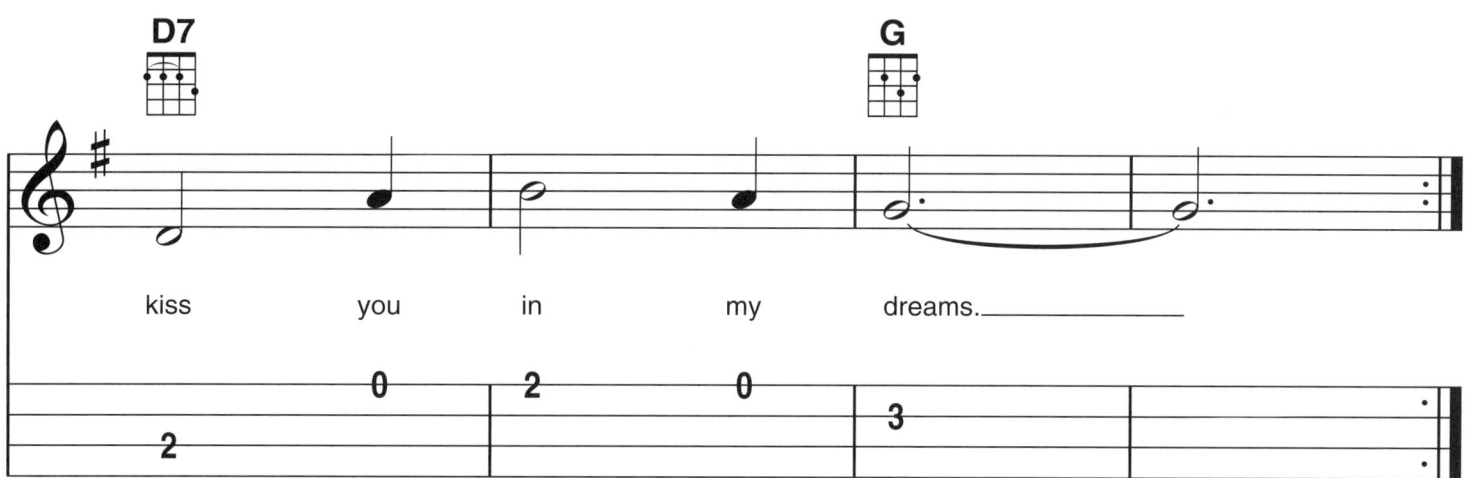

Additional Lyrics

2. Last Saturday night I got married.
   Me and my wife settled down.
   Now me and my wife are parted.
   I'm gonna take another stroll downtown.

3. Sometimes I live in the country.
   Sometimes I live in the town.
   Sometimes I have a great notion
   To jump into the river and drown.

4. Stop your rambling, stop your gambling.
   Stop your staying out late at night.
   Go home to your wife and family,
   By the fireplace, oh so bright.

Last Night I Had the Strangest Dream

Words and Music by
ED McCURDY

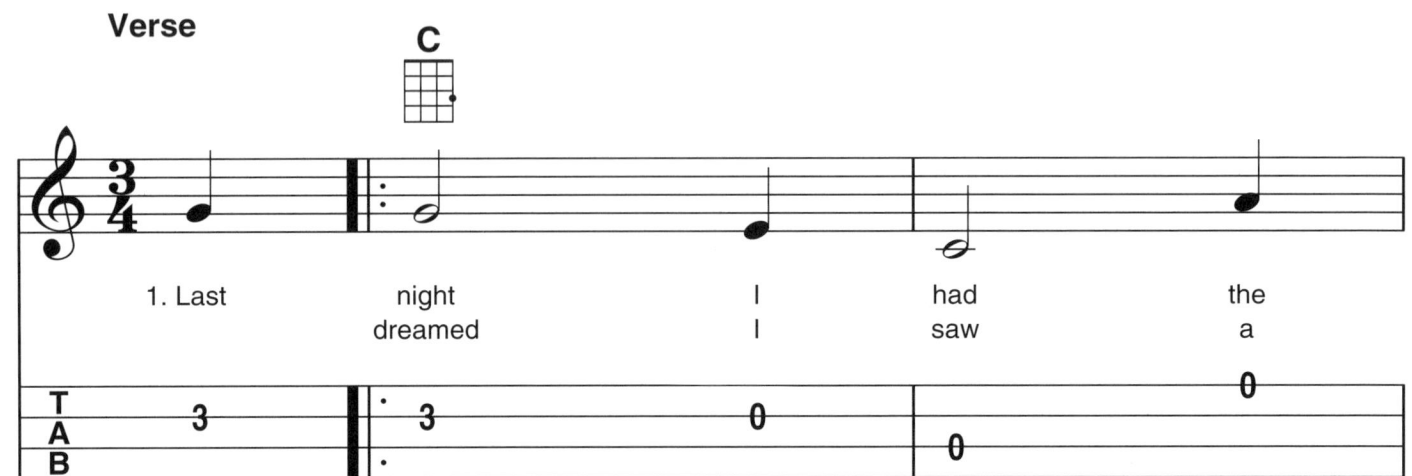
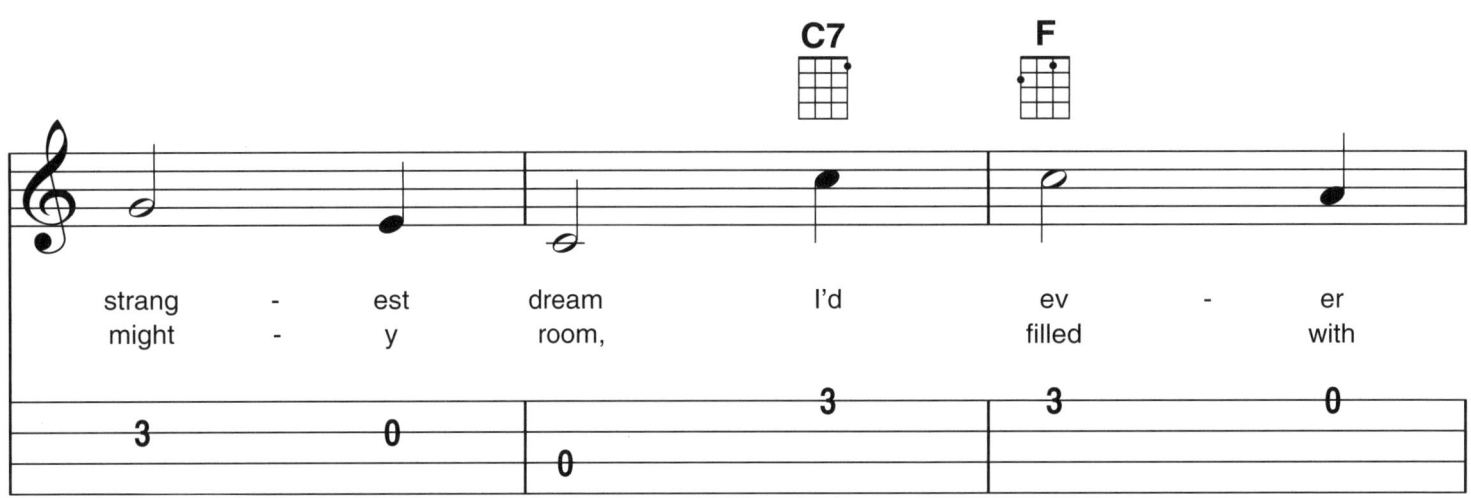
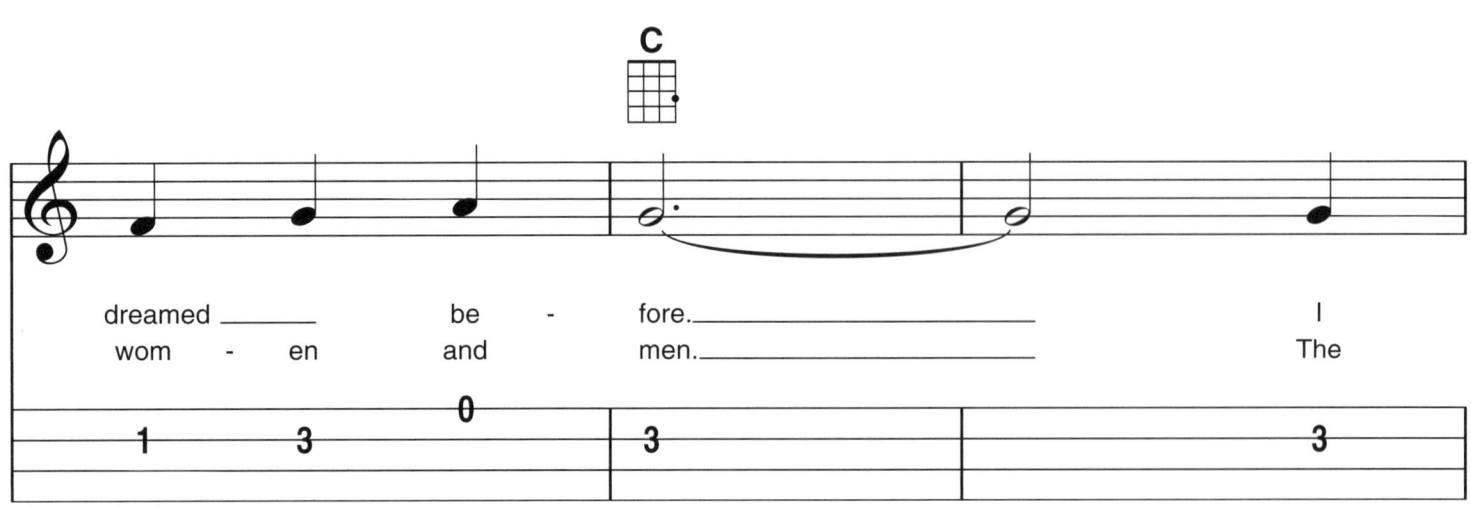

TRO - © Copyright 1950 (Renewed), 1951 (Renewed) and
1955 (Renewed) Folkways Music Publishers, Inc., New York, NY
International Copyright Secured
All Rights Reserved Including Public Performance For Profit
Used by Permission

Additional Lyrics

3. And when the paper was all signed,
   And a million copies made,
   They all joined hands and bowed their heads,
   And grateful prayers were prayed.

4. And people in the streets below,
   Were dancing 'round and 'round,
   While swords and guns and uniforms,
   Were scattered on the ground.

PASTURES OF PLENTY

Words and Music by
WOODY GUTHRIE

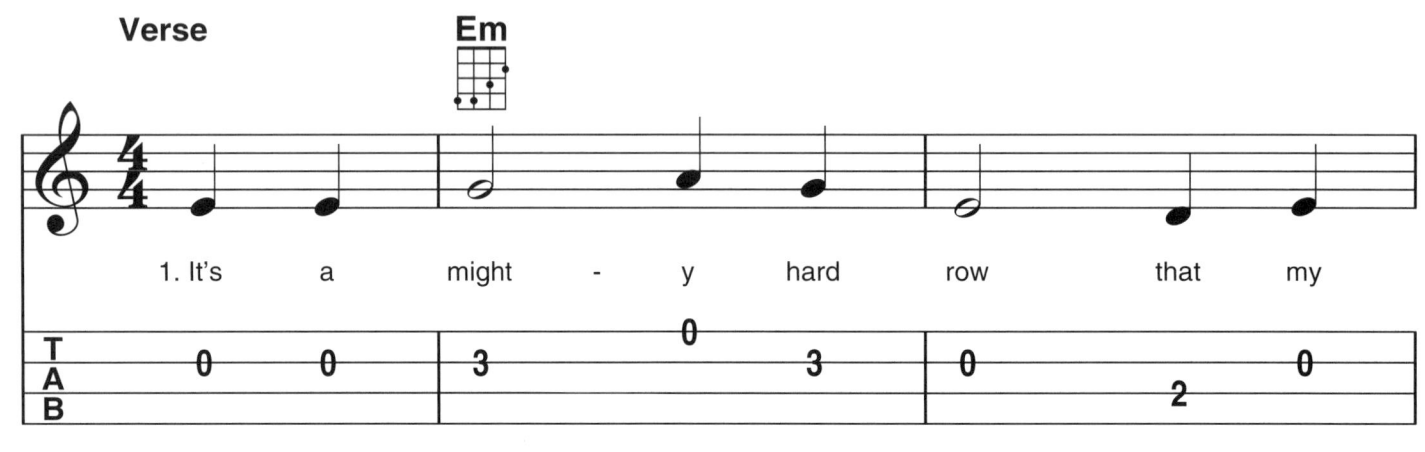

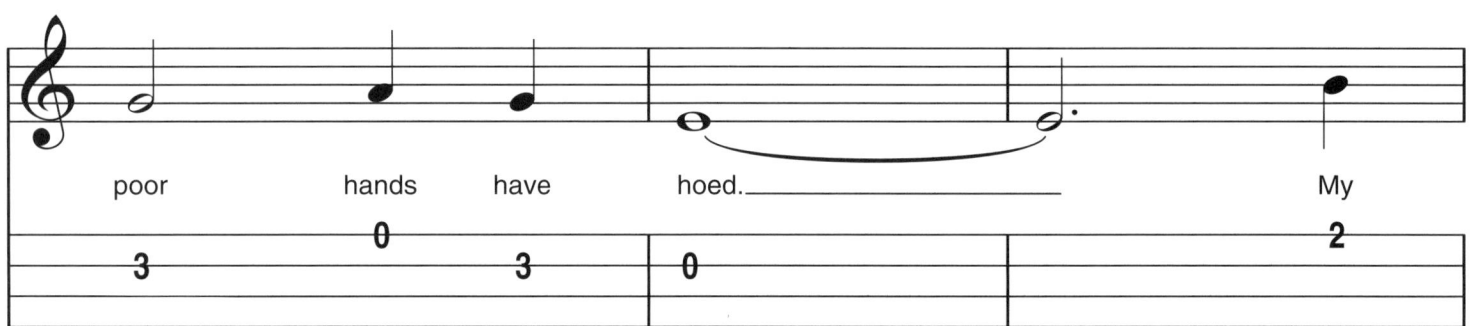

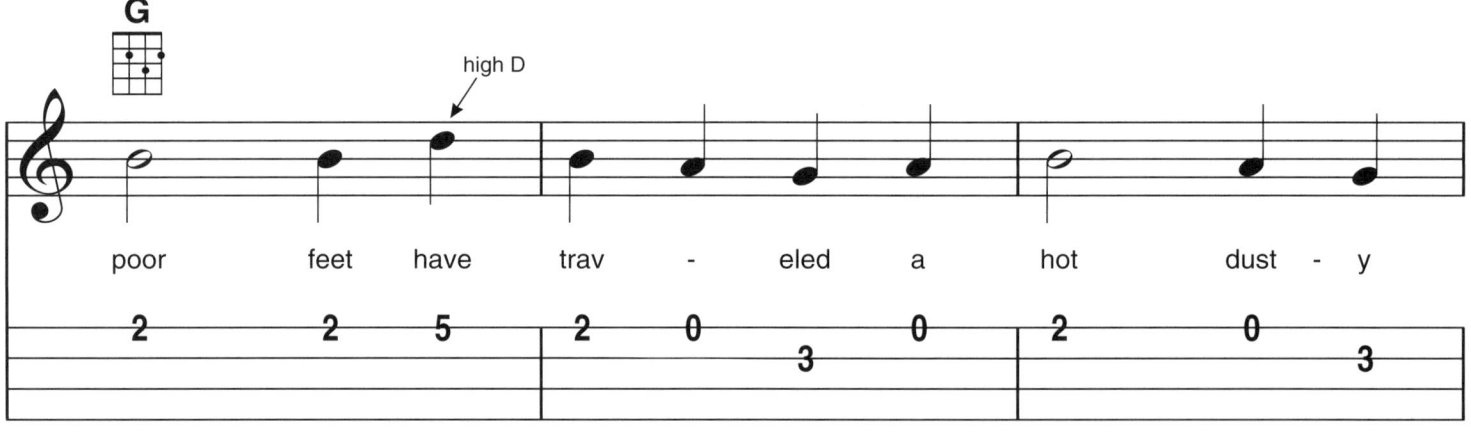

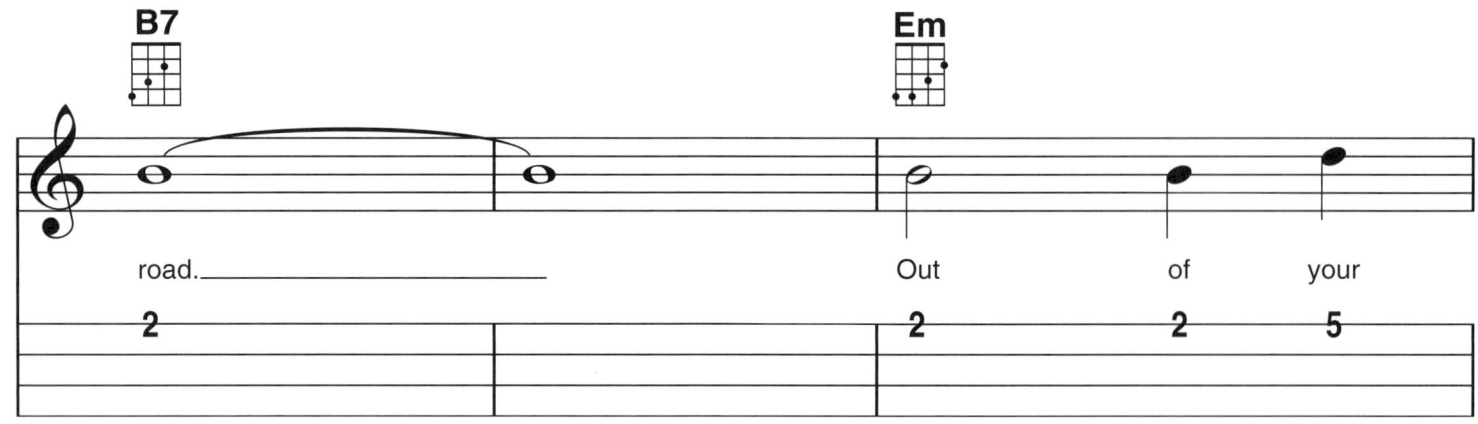

TRO - © Copyright 1960 (Renewed) and 1963 (Renewed) Ludlow Music, Inc., New York, NY
International Copyright Secured
All Rights Reserved Including Public Performance For Profit
Used by Permission

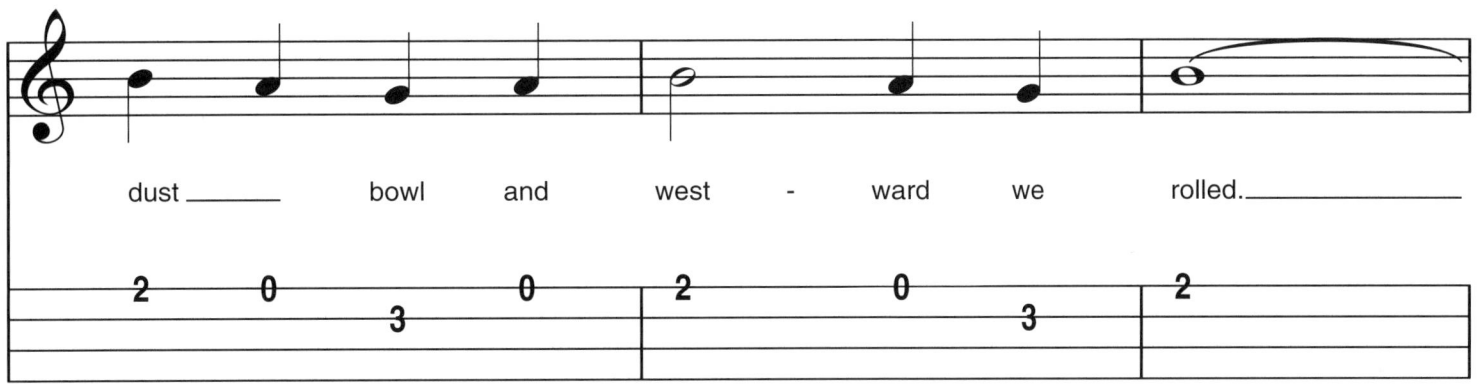
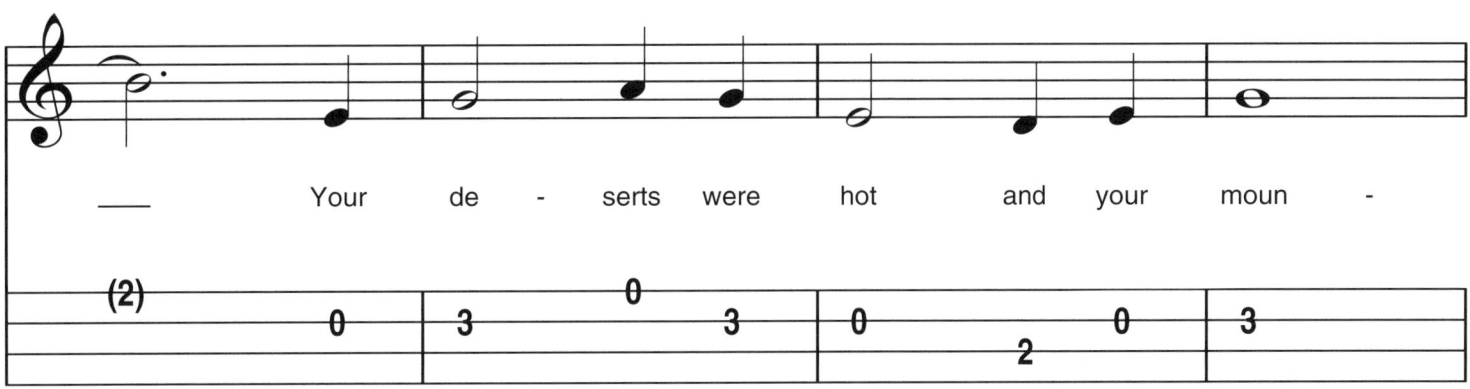
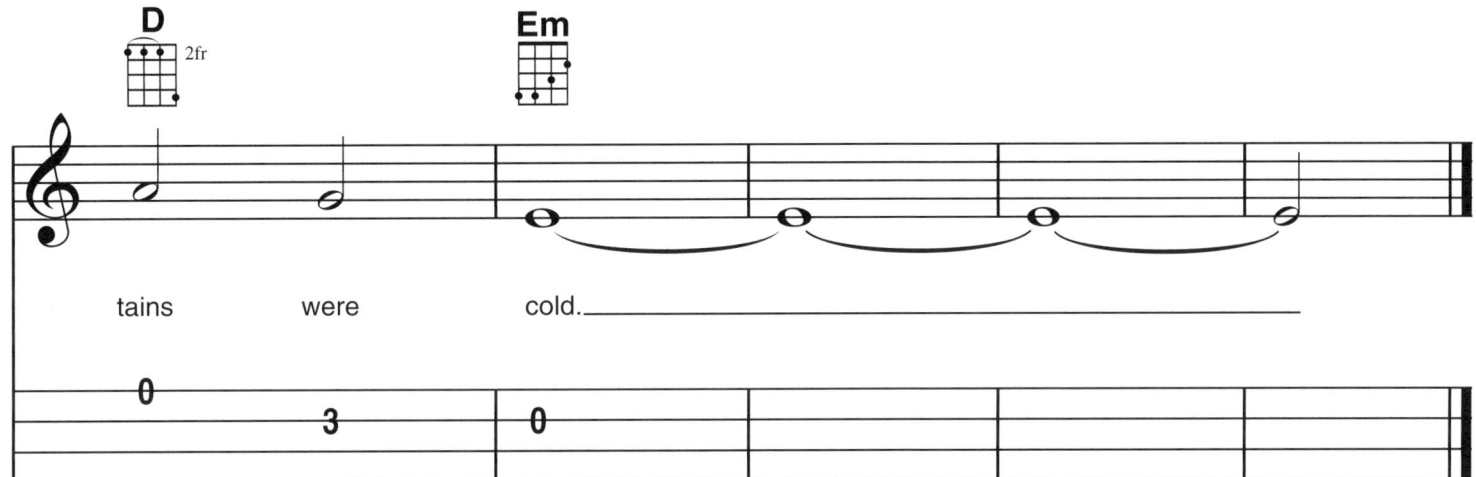

Additional Lyrics

2. I've worked in your orchards of peaches and prunes, slept on the ground in the light of the moon.
   On the edge of your city, you've seen us and then, we come with the dust and we go with the wind.

3. California and Arizona, I make all your crops, and it's north up to Oregon to gather your hops.
   Dig the beets from your ground, cut the grapes from your vine, to set on your table your light sparkling wine.

4. Green pastures of plenty from dry desert ground, from that Grand Coulee Dam where the waters run down.
   Every state in this union us migrants have been, we'll work in your fight and we'll fight 'til we win.

5. Well, it's always we ramble, that river and I, all along your green valley I'll work 'til I die.
   My land I'll defend with my life, if it be, 'cause my pastures of plenty must always be free.

I Walk the Line

Words and Music by
JOHN R. CASH

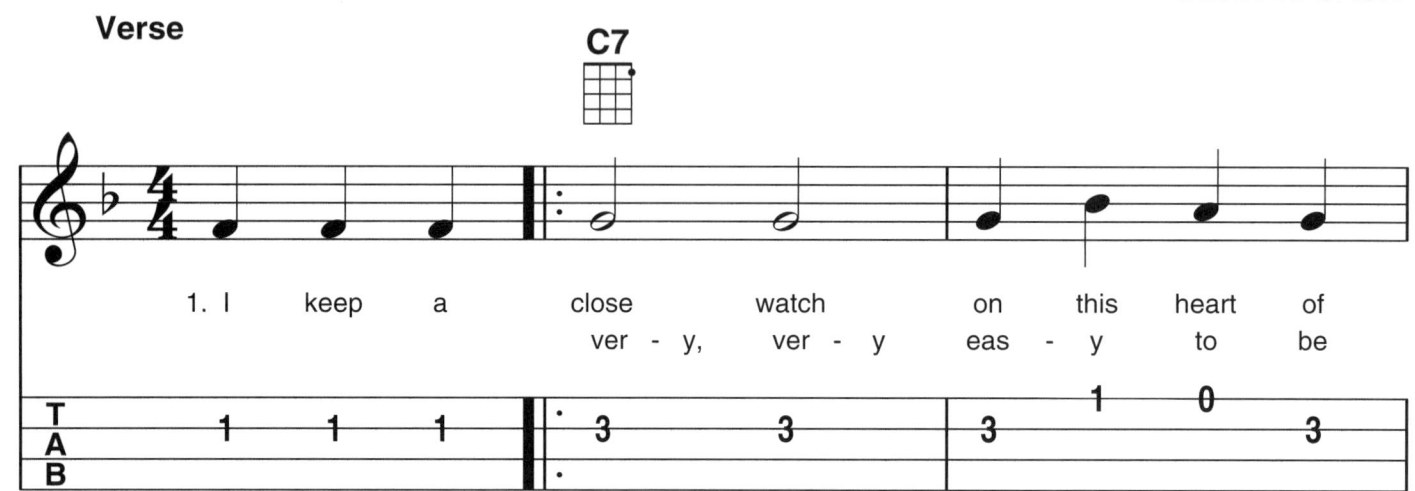
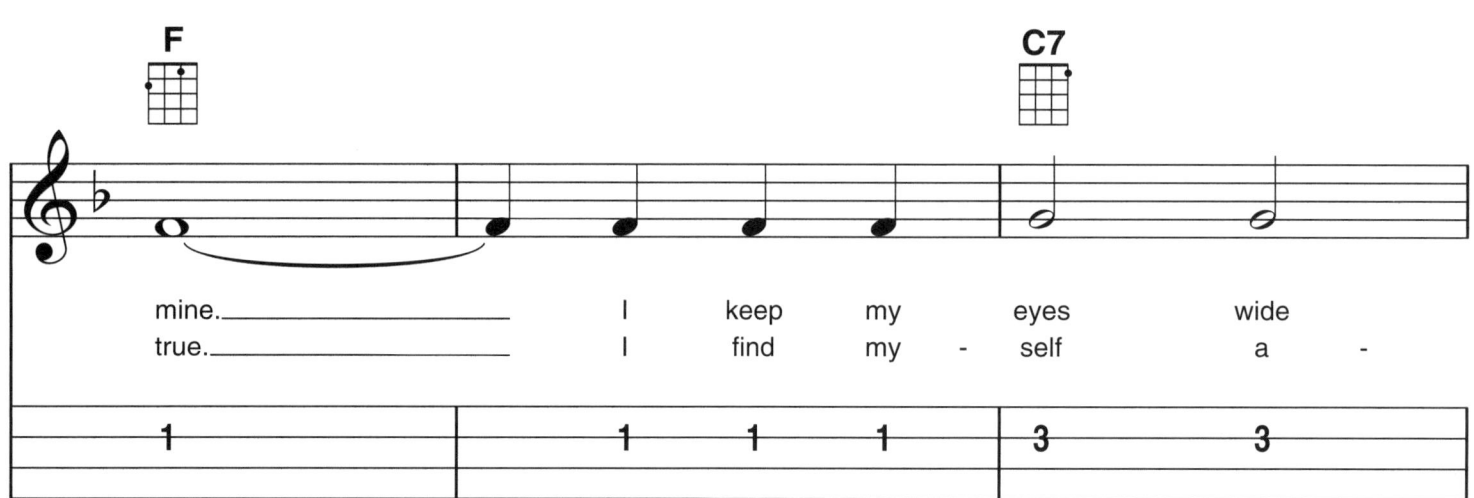
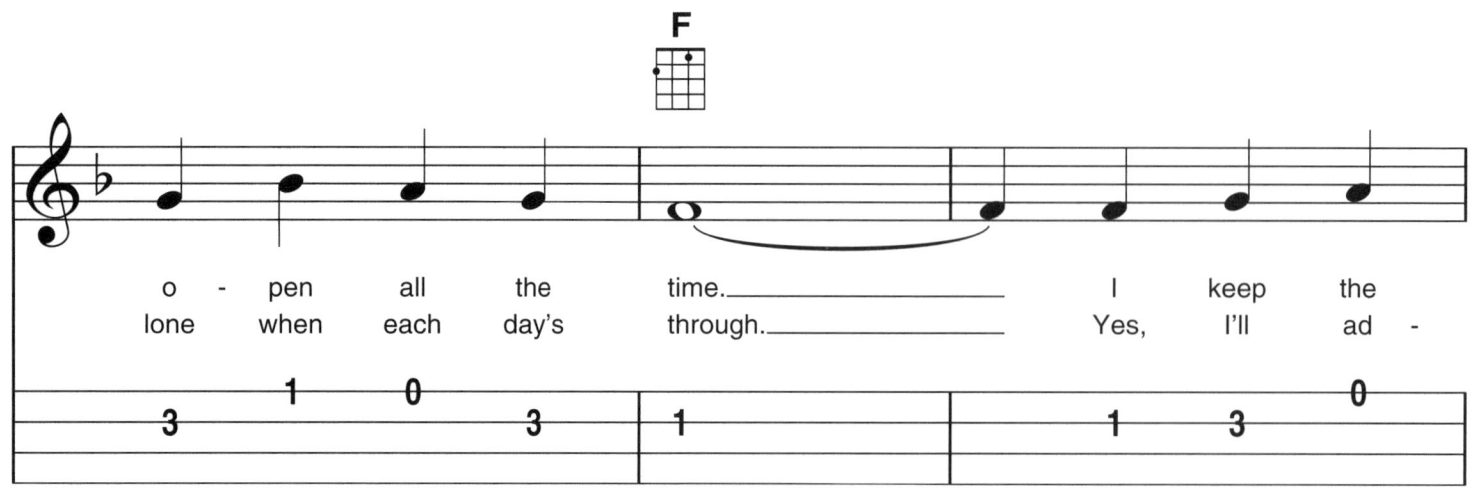

© 1956 (Renewed 1984) HOUSE OF CASH, INC. (BMI)/Administered by BUG MUSIC
All Rights Reserved   Used by Permission

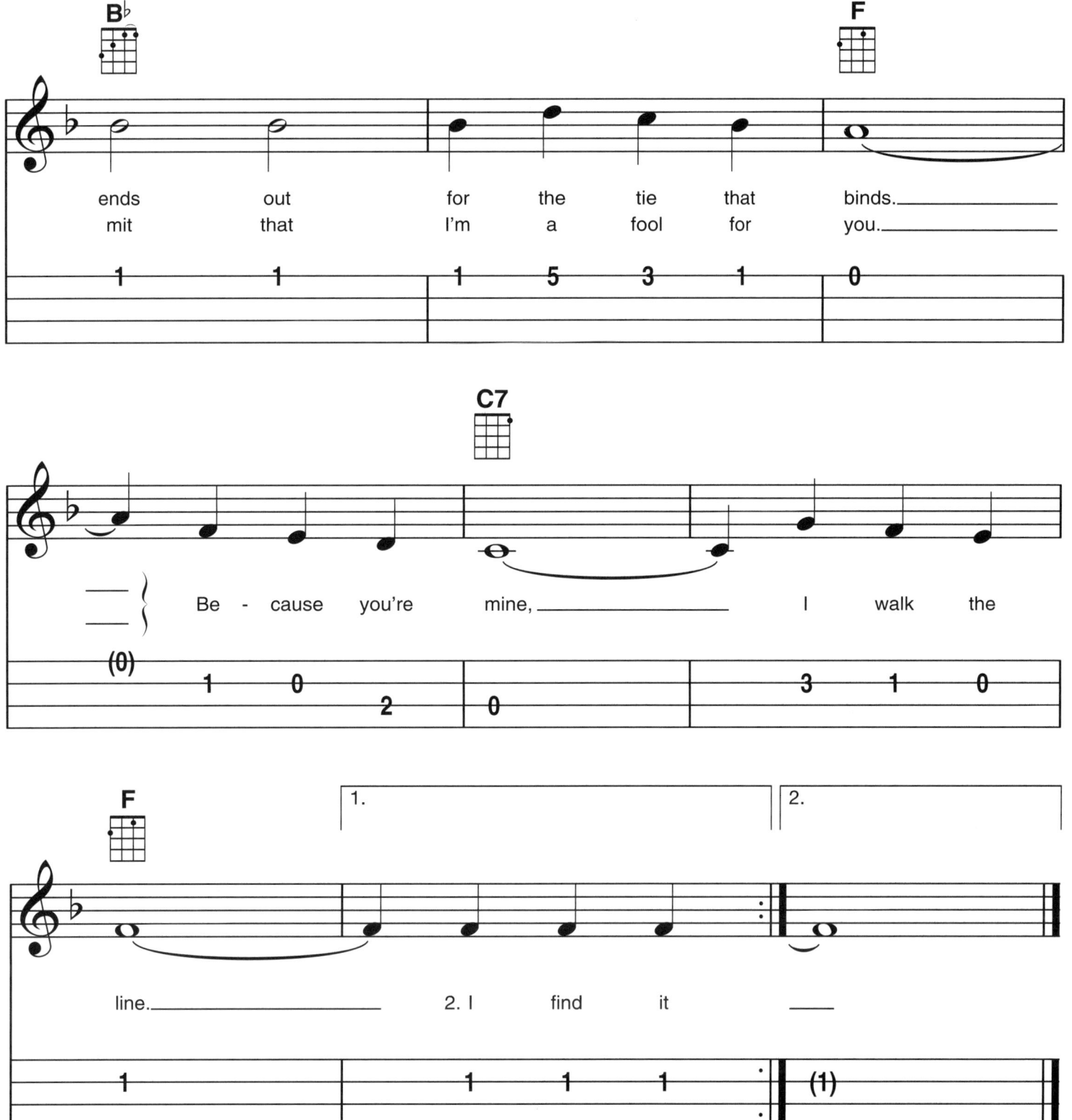

Additional Lyrics

3. As sure as night is dark and day is light, I keep you on my mind both day and night.
   And happiness I've known proves that it's right. Because you're mine, I walk the line.

4. You've got a way to keep me on your side. You give me cause for love that I can't hide.
   For you I know I'd even try to turn the tide. Because you're mine, I walk the line.

5. I keep a close watch on this heart of mine. I keep my eyes wide open all the time.
   I keep the ends out for the tie that binds. Because you're mine, I walk the line.

THE HOUSE OF THE RISING SUN

Words and Music by
ALAN PRICE

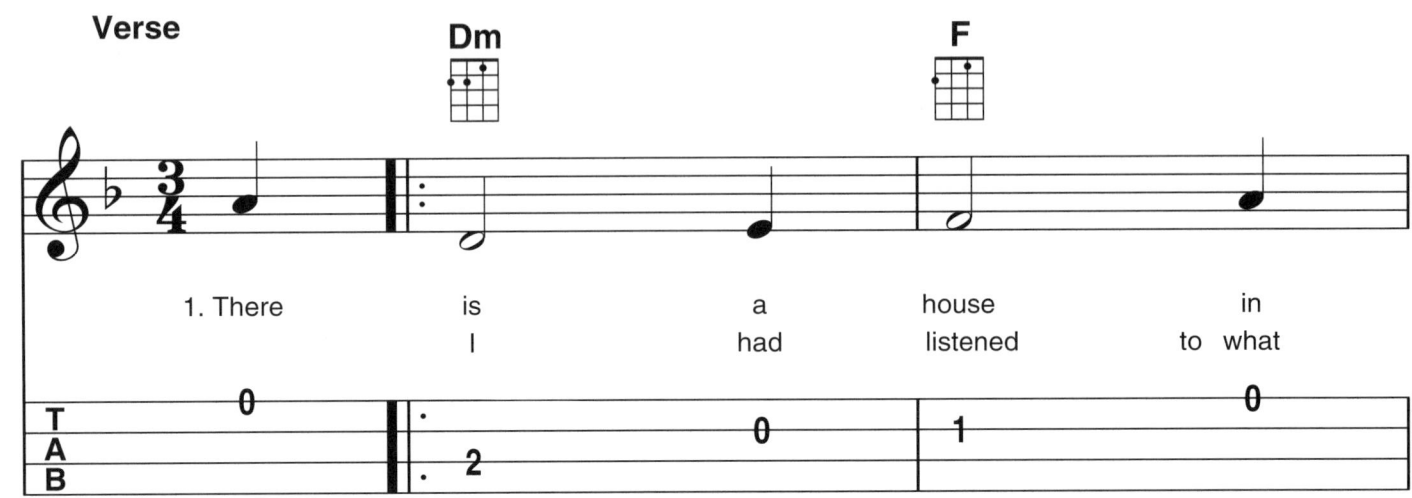
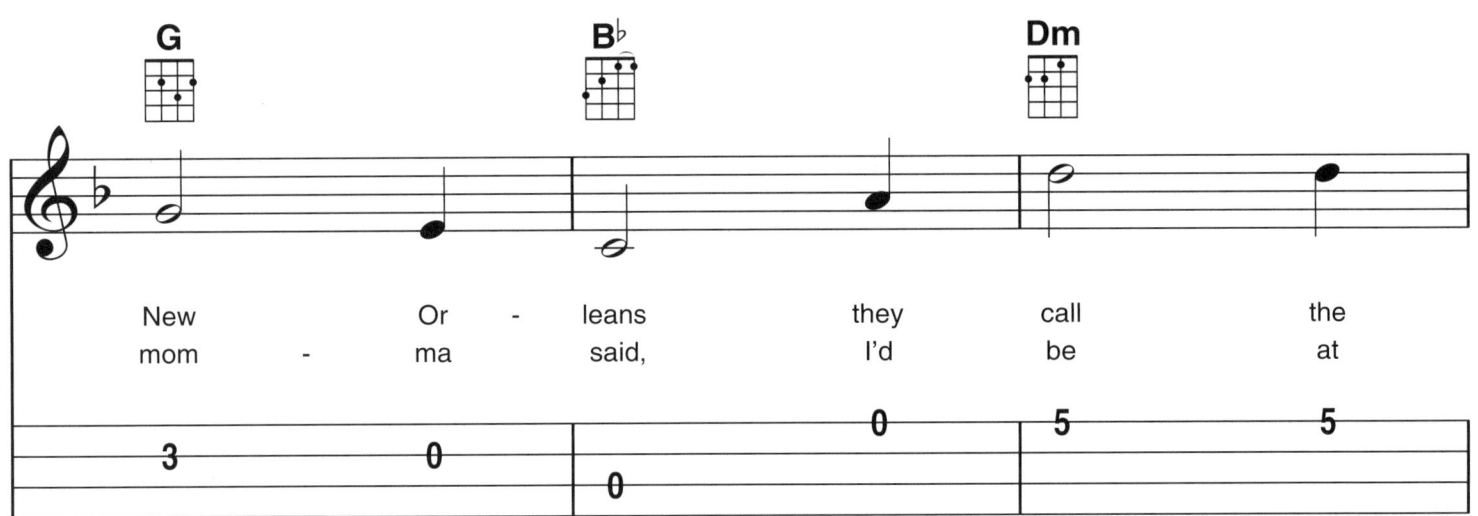
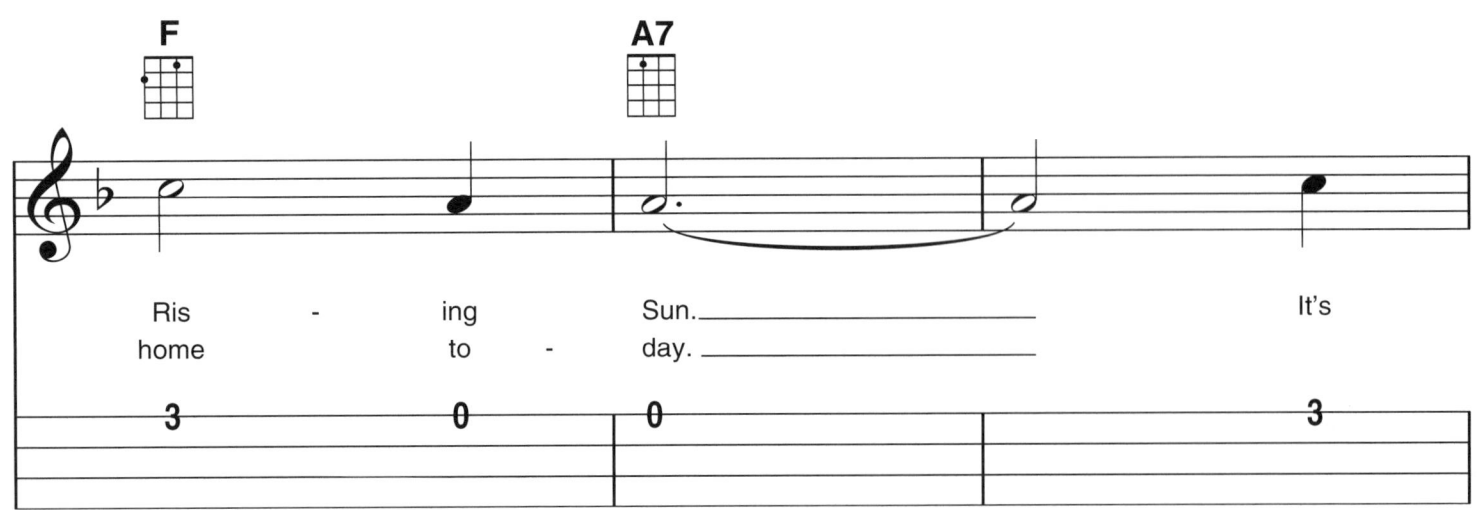

© 1964 (Renewed 1992) KEITH PROWSE MUSIC PUBLISHING CO., LTD.
All Rights Reserved   International Copyright Secured   Used by Permission

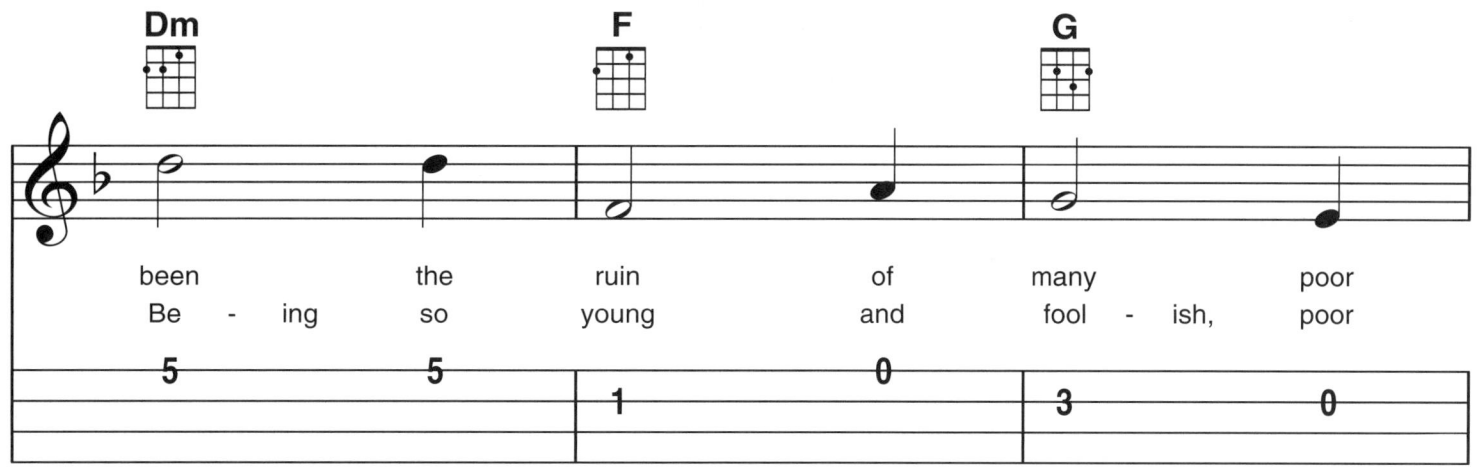
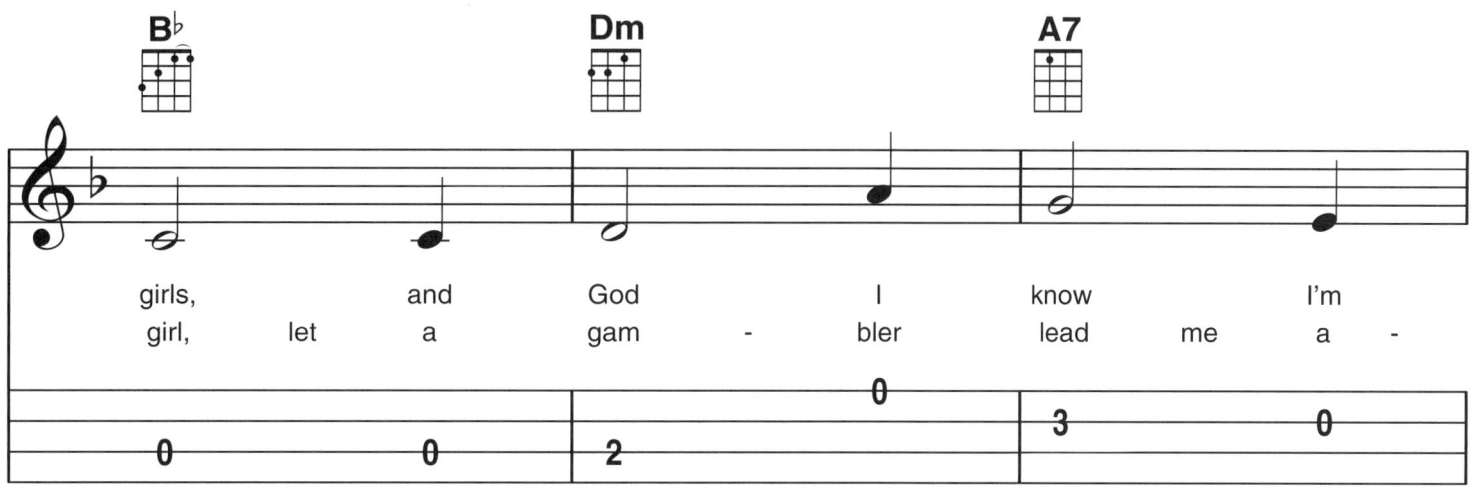
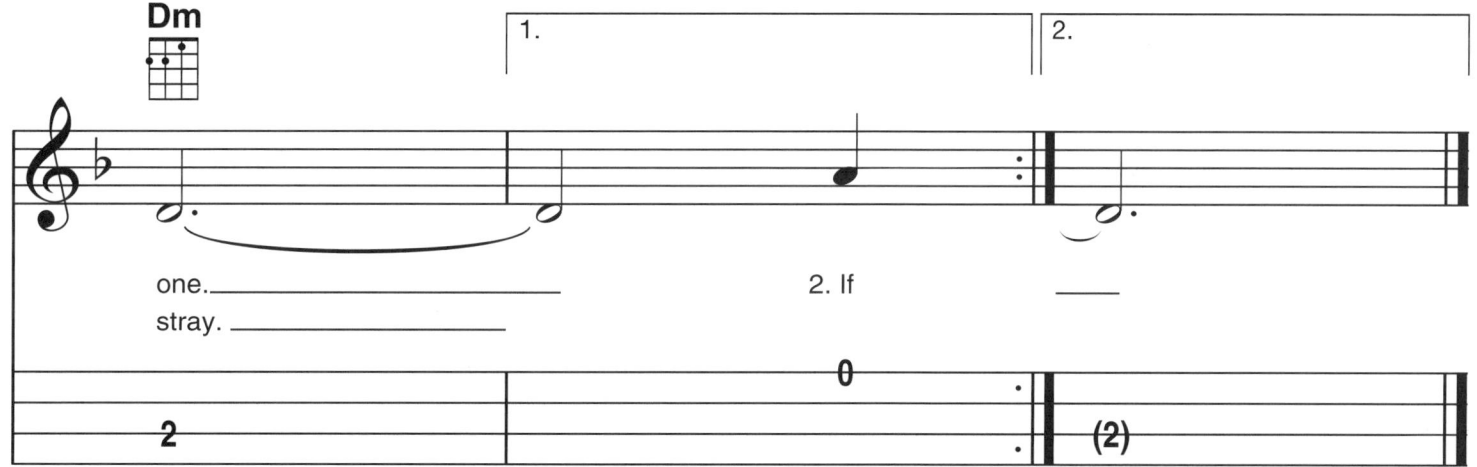

Additional Lyrics

3. The only thing a gambler needs is a suitcase and a trunk,
   And the only time he's satisfied is when he's all a-drunk.

4. Go tell my baby sister never do like I have done.
   To shun that house in New Orleans they call the Rising Sun.

5. I'm going back to New Orleans, my race is almost run.
   Going back to end my life beneath the Rising Sun.

This Land Is Your Land

Words and Music by
WOODY GUTHRIE

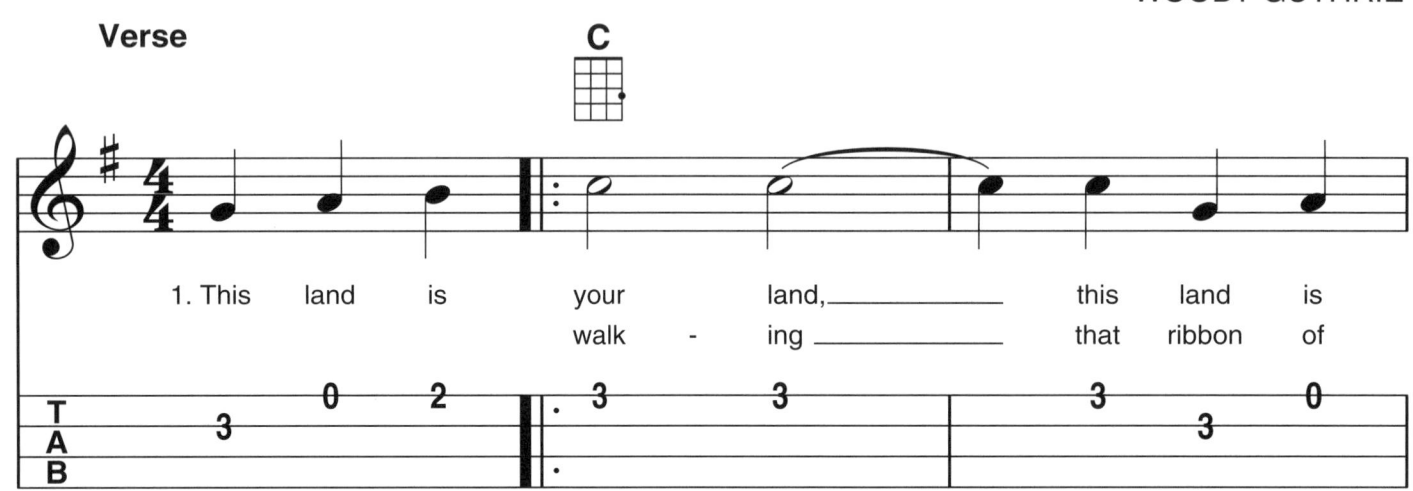
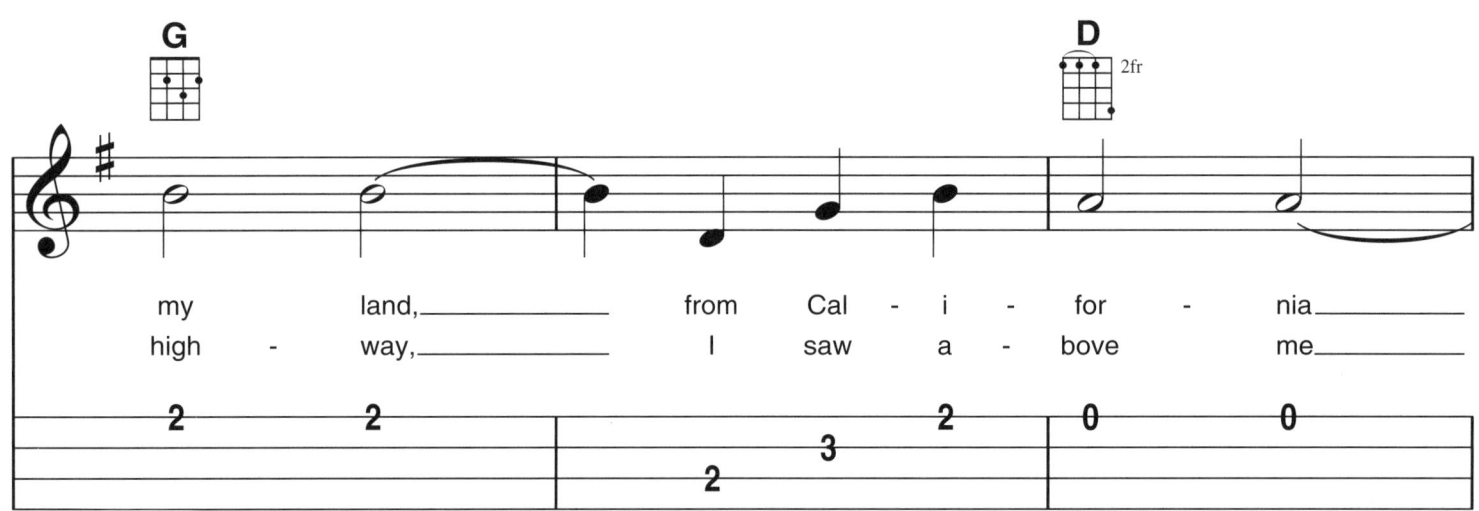
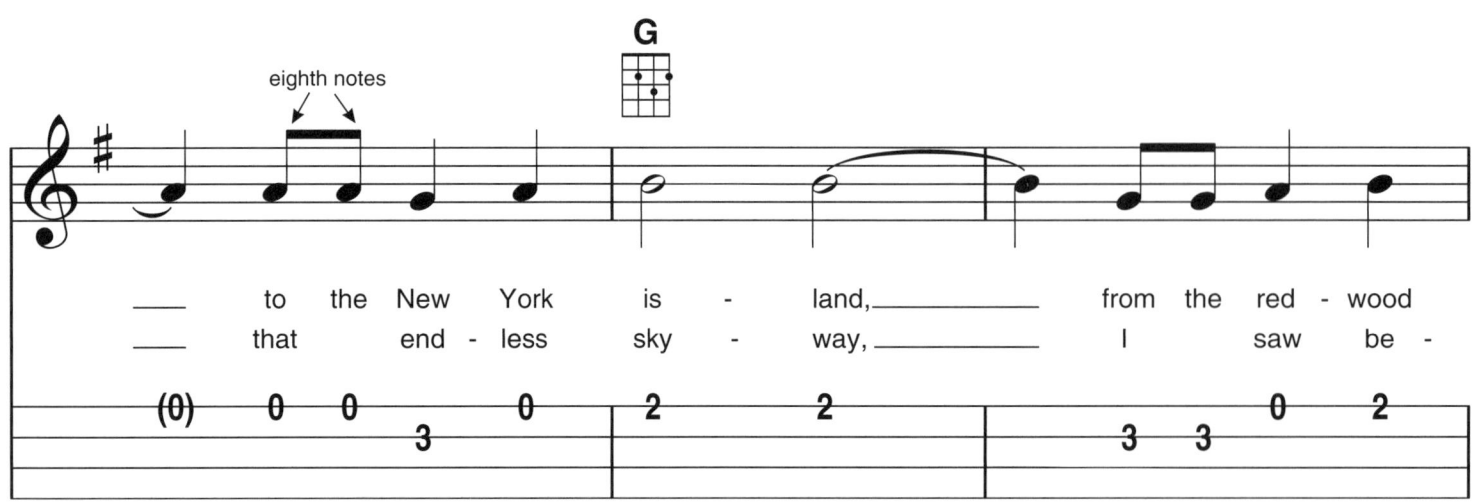

TRO - © Copyright 1956 (Renewed), 1958 (Renewed), 1970 (Renewed)
and 1972 (Renewed) Ludlow Music, Inc., New York, NY
International Copyright Secured
All Rights Reserved Including Public Performance For Profit
Used by Permission

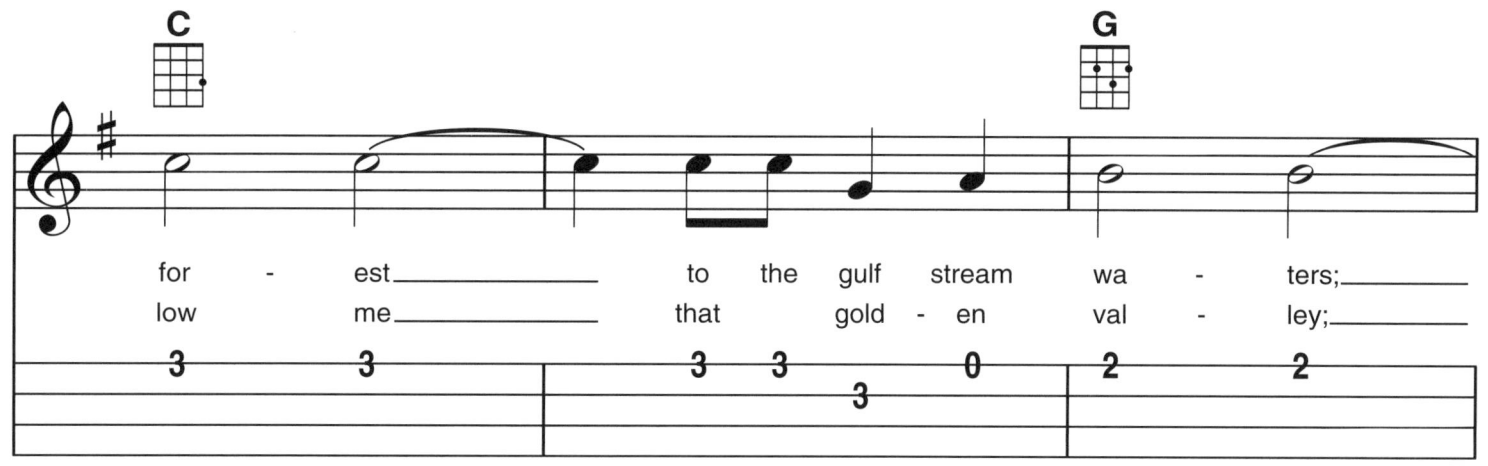
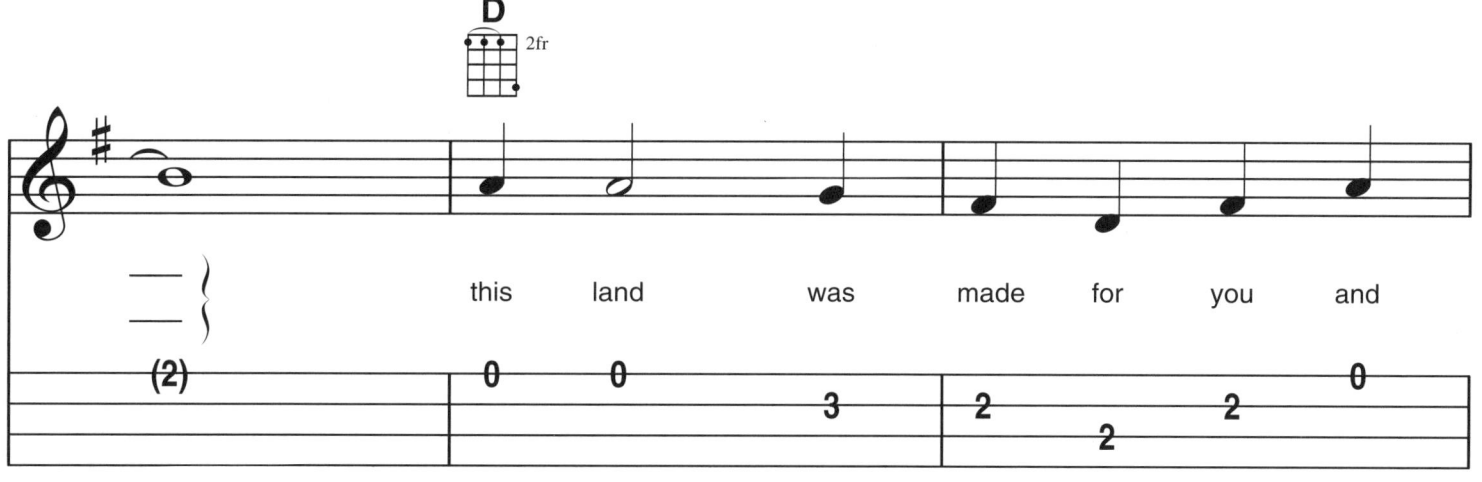

Additional Lyrics

3. I've roamed and rambled, and I followed my footsteps
   To the sparkling sands of her diamond deserts.
   And all around me a voice was sounding,
   "This land was made for you and me."

4. When the sun comes shining, and I was strolling,
   And the wheat fields waving, and the dust clouds rolling.
   As the fog was lifting a voice was chanting,
   "This land was made for you and me."

5. In the shadow of the steeple I saw my people,
   By the relief office I seen my people.
   As they stood there hungry, I stood there asking,
   "Is this land made for you and me?"

6. Nobody living can ever stop me
   As I go walking down that freedom highway,
   Nobody living can ever make me turn back.
   This land was made for you and me.

I'M SO LONESOME I COULD CRY

Words and Music by
HANK WILLIAMS

Copyright © 1949 Sony/ATV Music Publishing LLC and Hiriam Music in the U.S.A.
Copyright Renewed
All Rights on behalf of Hiriam Music Administered by Rightsong Music Inc.
All Rights outside the U.S.A. Controlled by Sony/ATV Music Publishing LLC
All Rights on behalf of Sony/ATV Music Publishing LLC Administered by Sony/ATV Music Publishing LLC, 8 Music Square West, Nashville, TN 37203
International Copyright Secured   All Rights Reserved

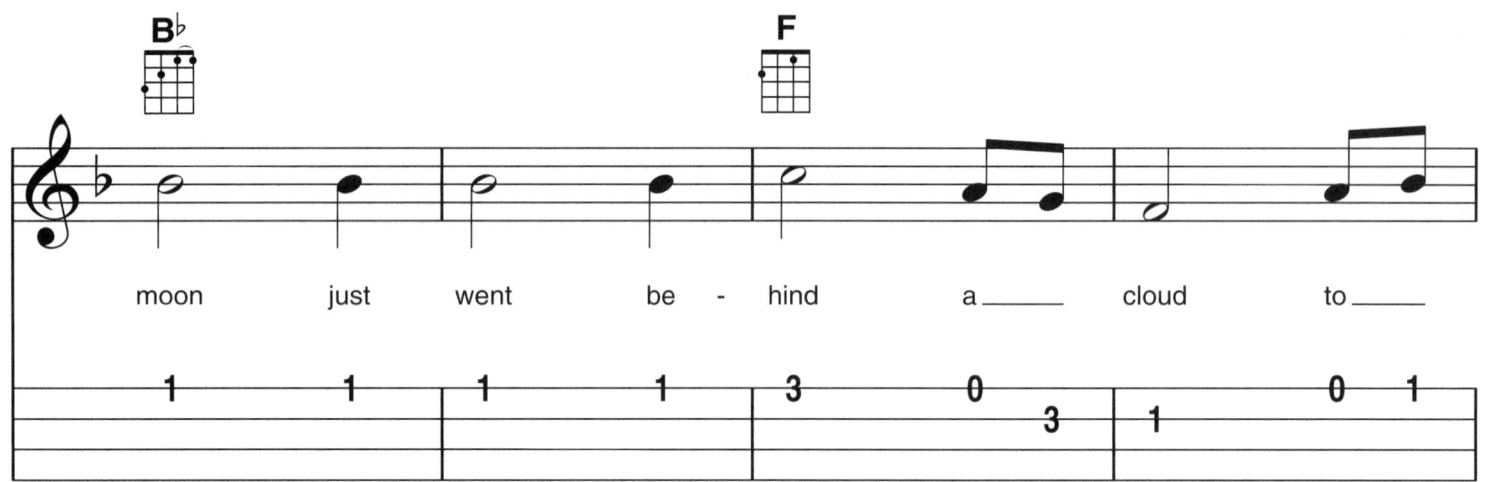
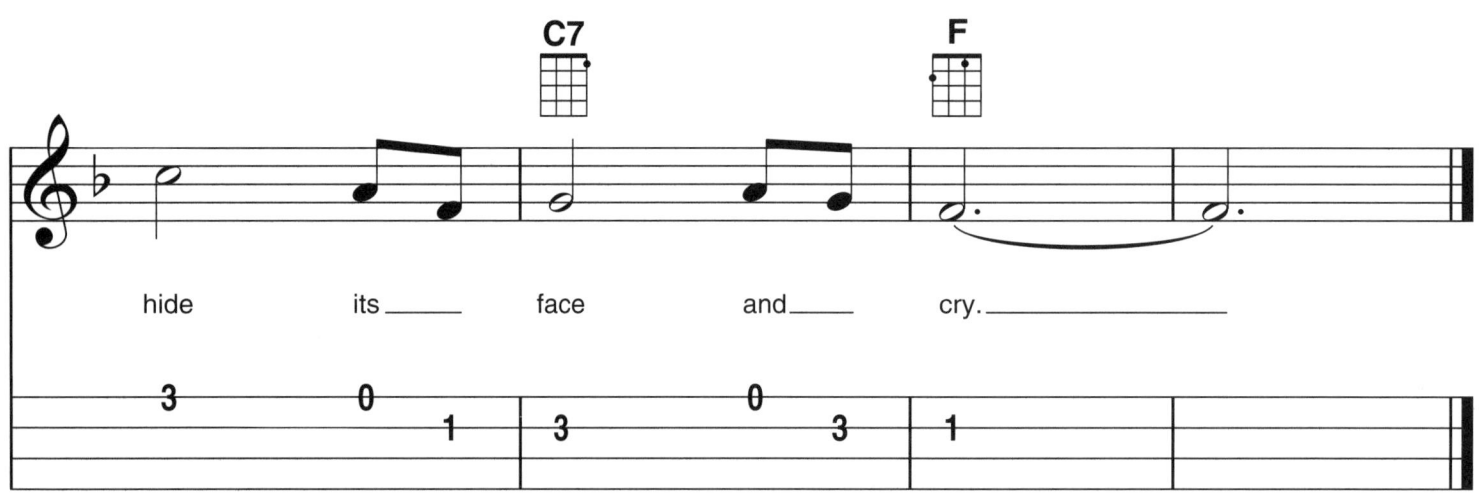

Additional Lyrics

3. Did you ever see a robin weep,
   When leaves began to die?
   That means he's lost the will to live,
   I'm so lonesome I could cry.

4. The silence of a falling star
   Lights up a purple sky.
   And as I wonder where you are,
   I'm so lonesome I could cry.

We Shall Overcome

Inspired by African American Gospel Singing, members of the Food and Tobacco Workers Union, Charleston, SC, and the southern Civil Rights Movement

Musical and Lyrical Adaptation by
ZILPHIA HORTON, FRANK HAMILTON,
GUY CARAWAN and PETE SEEGER

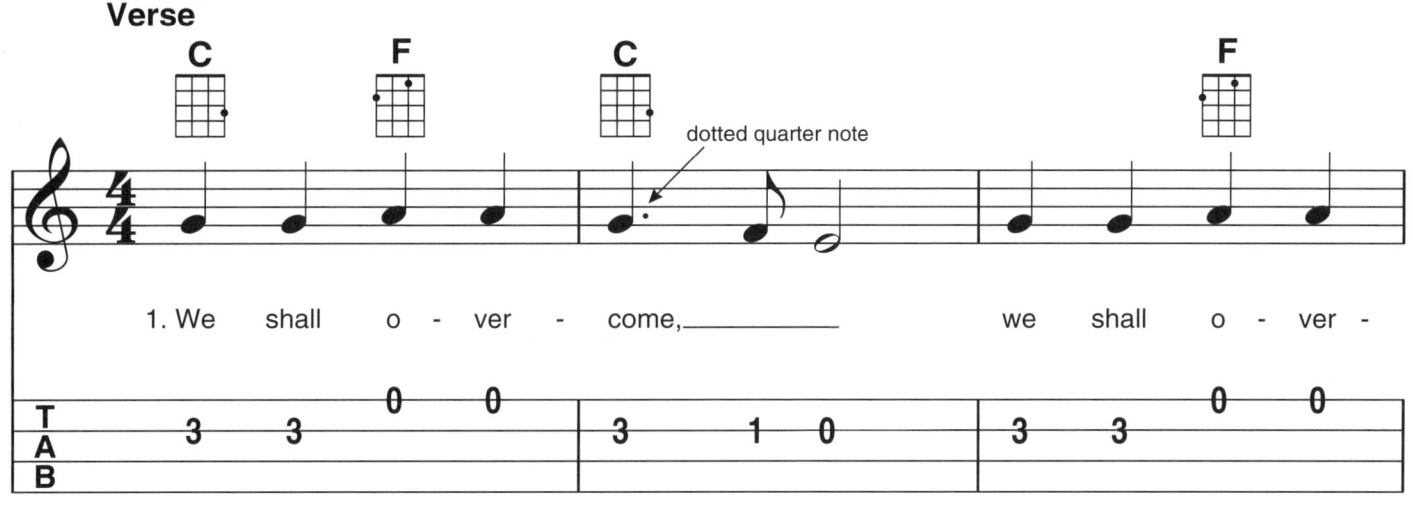
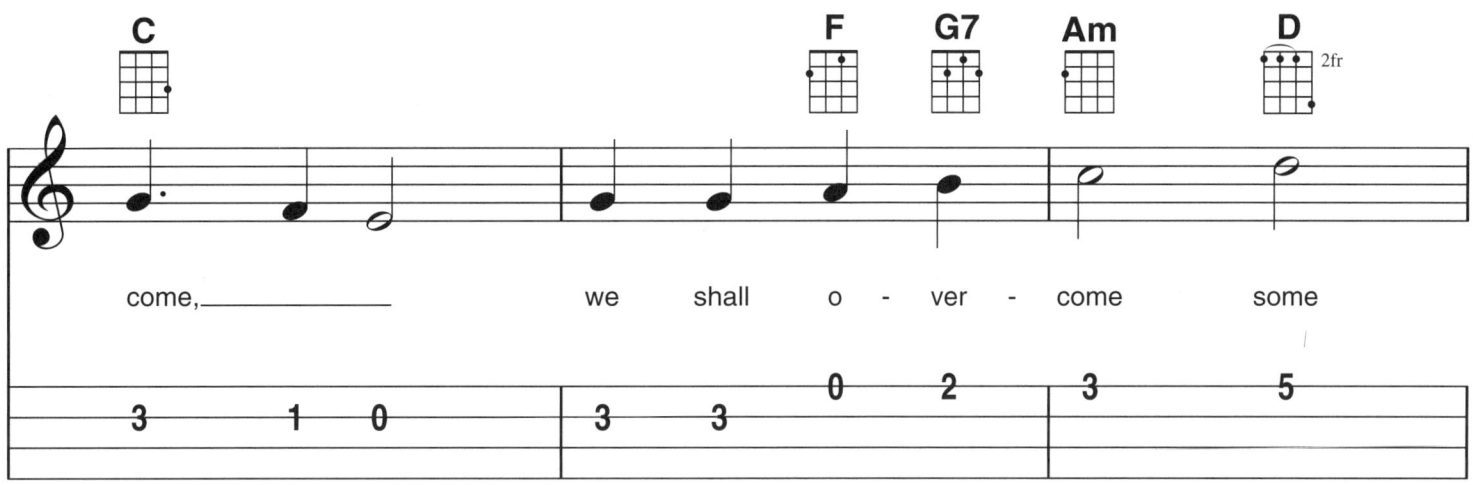
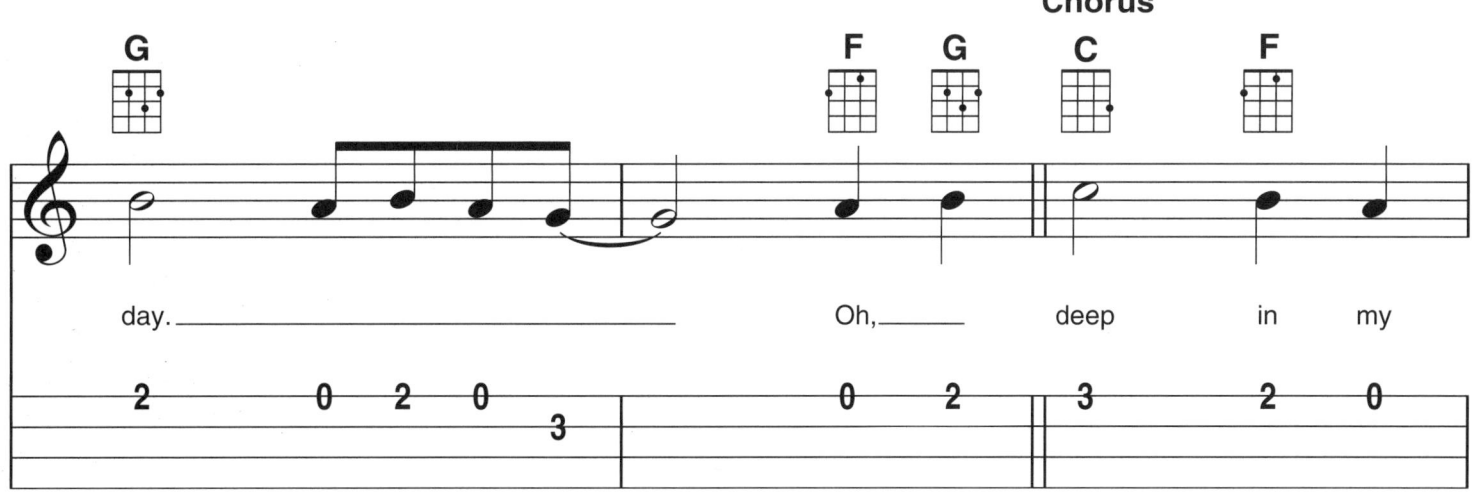

TRO - © Copyright 1960 (Renewed) and 1963 (Renewed) Ludlow Music, Inc., New York, NY
International Copyright Secured
All Rights Reserved Including Public Performance For Profit
Used by Permission
Royalties derived from this composition are being contributed to the We Shall Overcome Fund
and The Freedom Movement under the Trusteeship of the writers.

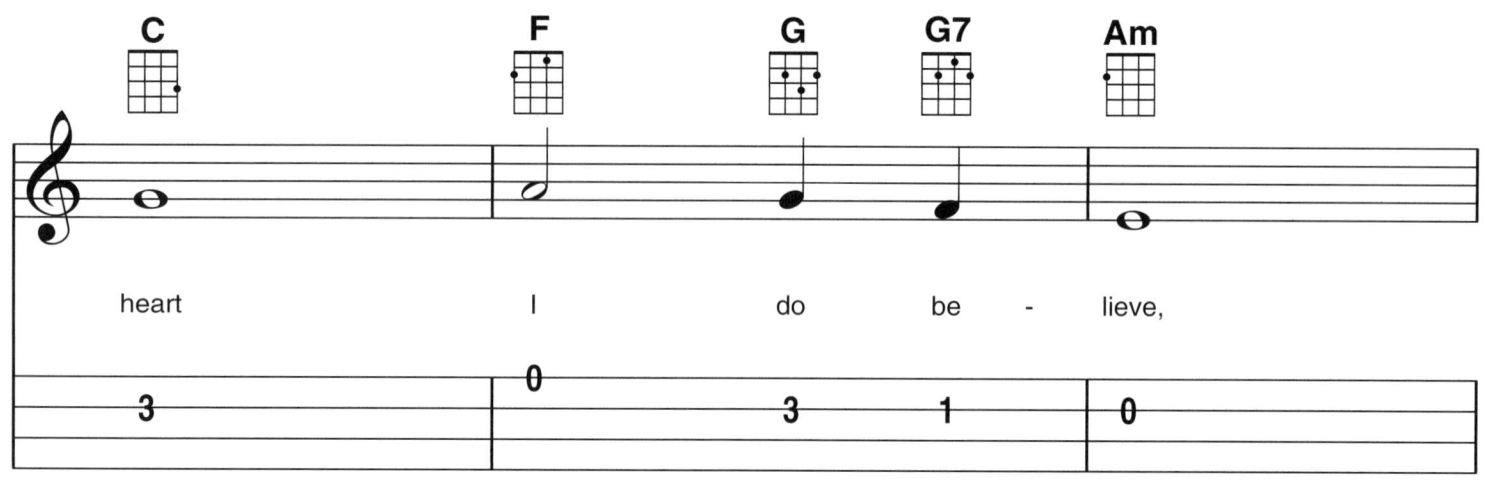
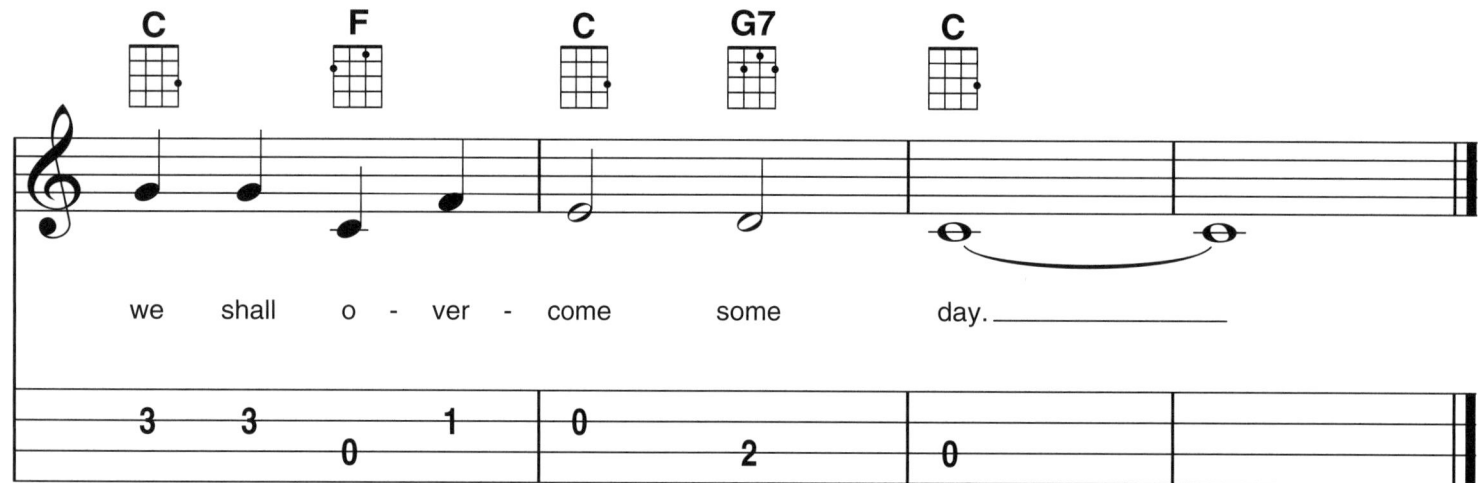

Additional Lyrics

2. We'll walk hand in hand,
   We'll walk hand in hand,
   We'll walk hand in hand some day.

3. We shall live in peace,
   We shall live in peace,
   We shall live in peace some day.

4. We shall all be free,
   We shall all be free,
   We shall all be free some day.

5. We are not afraid,
   We are not afraid,
   We are not afraid, today.

6. We shall overcome,
   We shall overcome,
   We shall overcome some day.

Your Cheatin' Heart

Words and Music by
HANK WILLIAMS

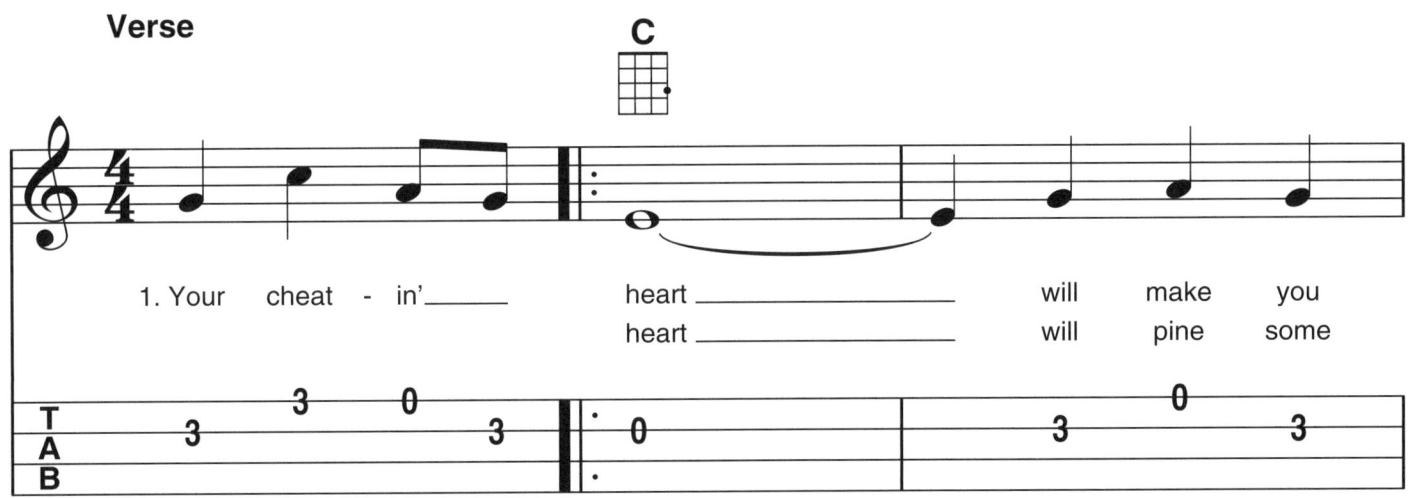

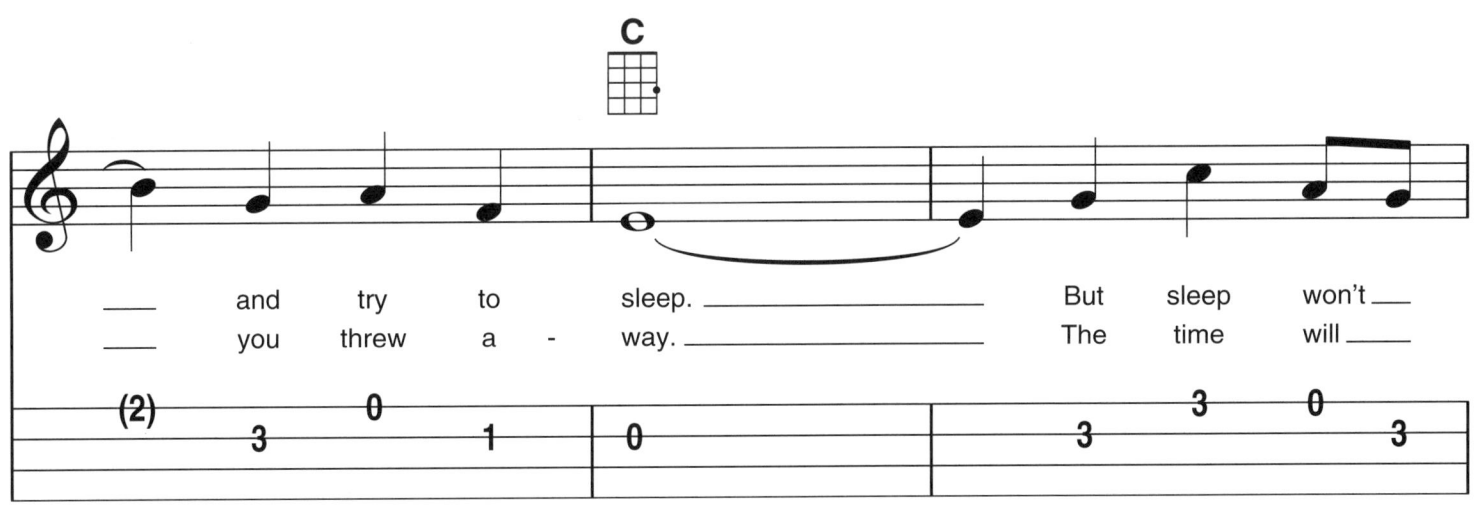

Copyright © 1952 Sony/ATV Music Publishing LLC and Hiriam Music in the U.S.A.
Copyright Renewed
All Rights on behalf of Hiriam Music Administered by Rightsong Music Inc.
All Rights outside the U.S.A. Controlled by Sony/ATV Music Publishing LLC
All Rights on behalf of Sony/ATV Music Publishing LLC Administered by Sony/ATV Music Publishing LLC, 8 Music Square West, Nashville, TN 37203
International Copyright Secured   All Rights Reserved

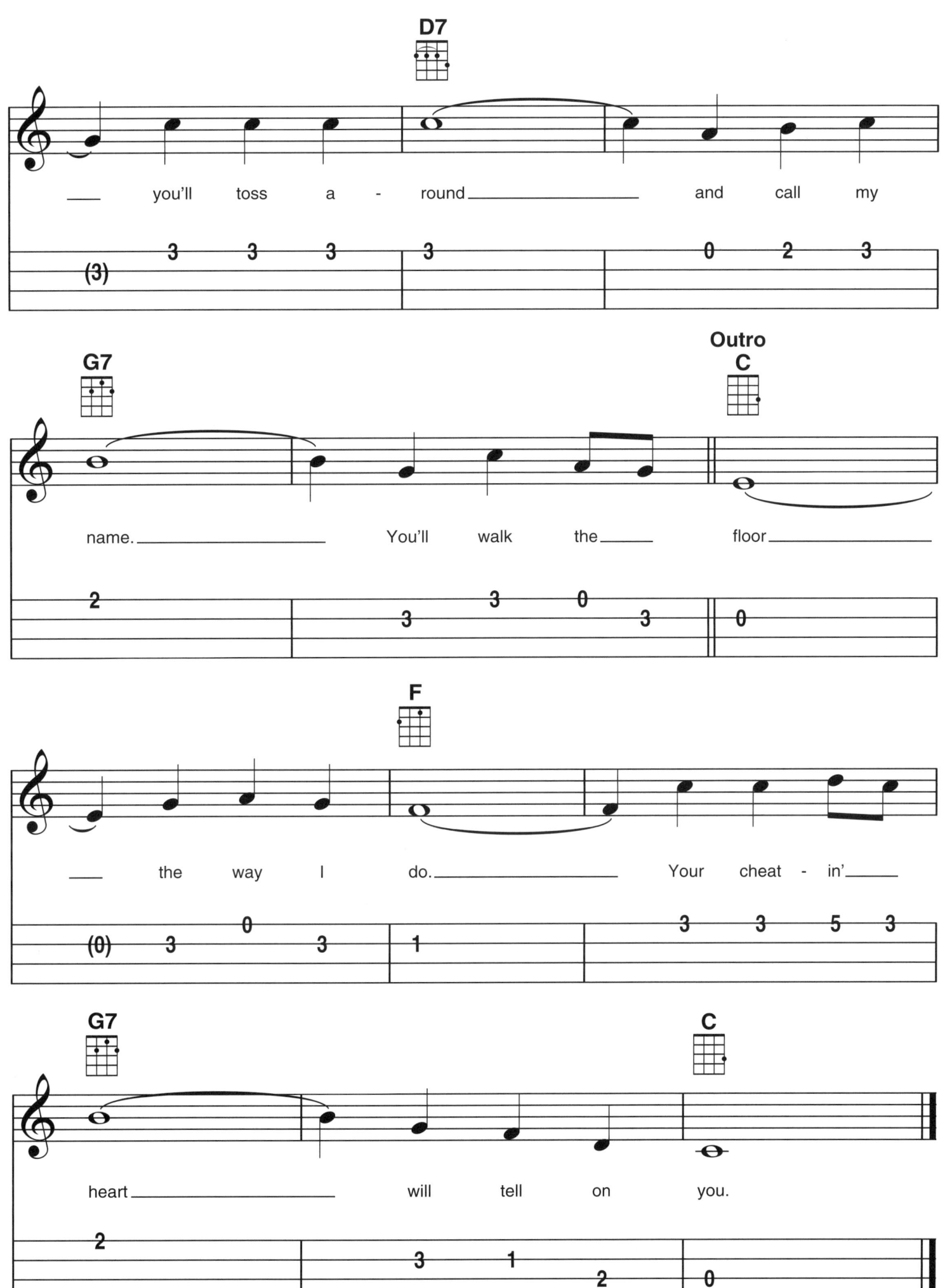

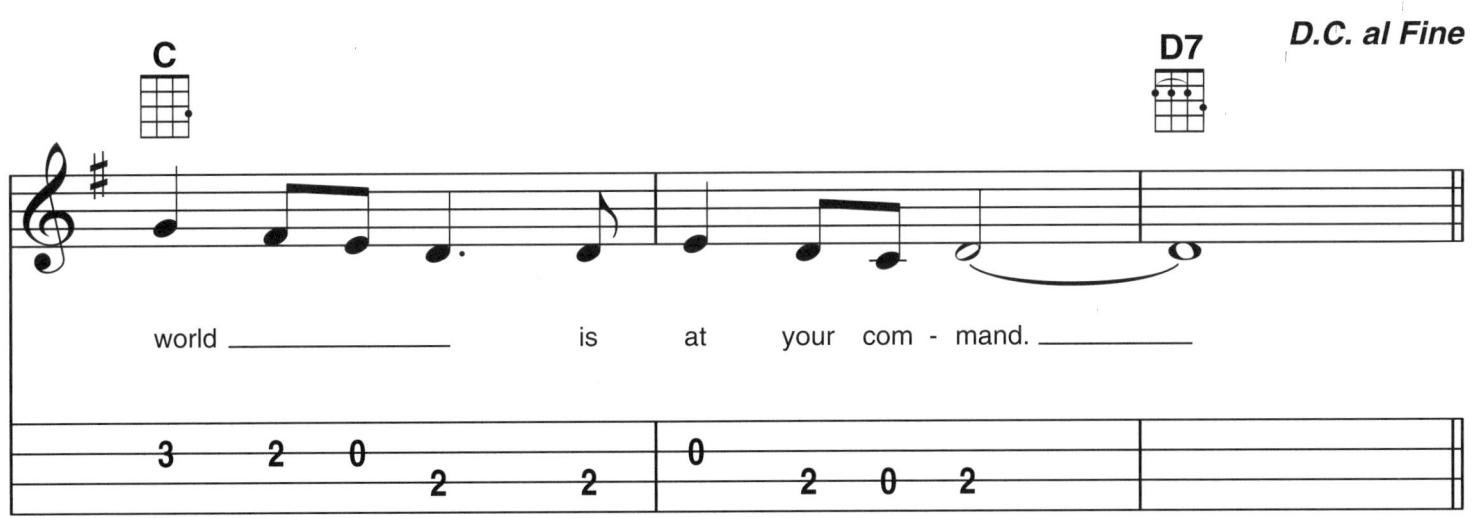

Additional Lyrics

2. He's as blind as he can be, just sees what he wants to see.
   Nowhere man can you see me at all?
   Nowhere man, don't worry. Take your time, don't hurry.
   Leave it all till somebody else lends you a hand.

OB-LA-DI, OB-LA-DA

Words and Music by
JOHN LENNON and PAUL McCARTNEY

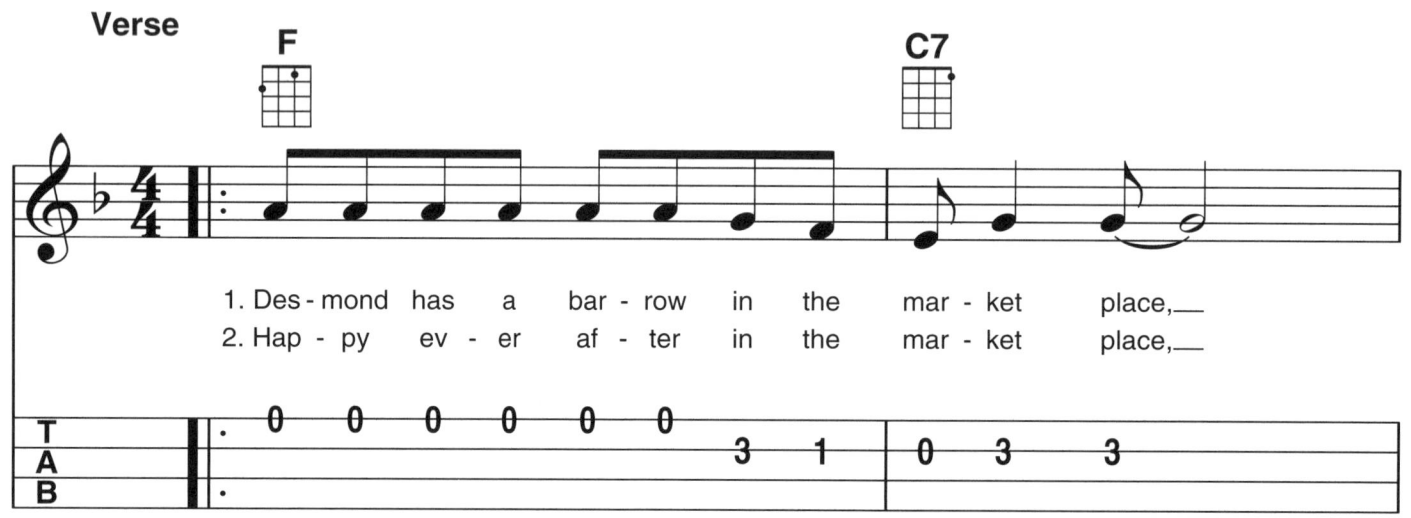

1. Des-mond has a bar-row in the mar-ket place,
2. Hap-py ev-er af-ter in the mar-ket place,

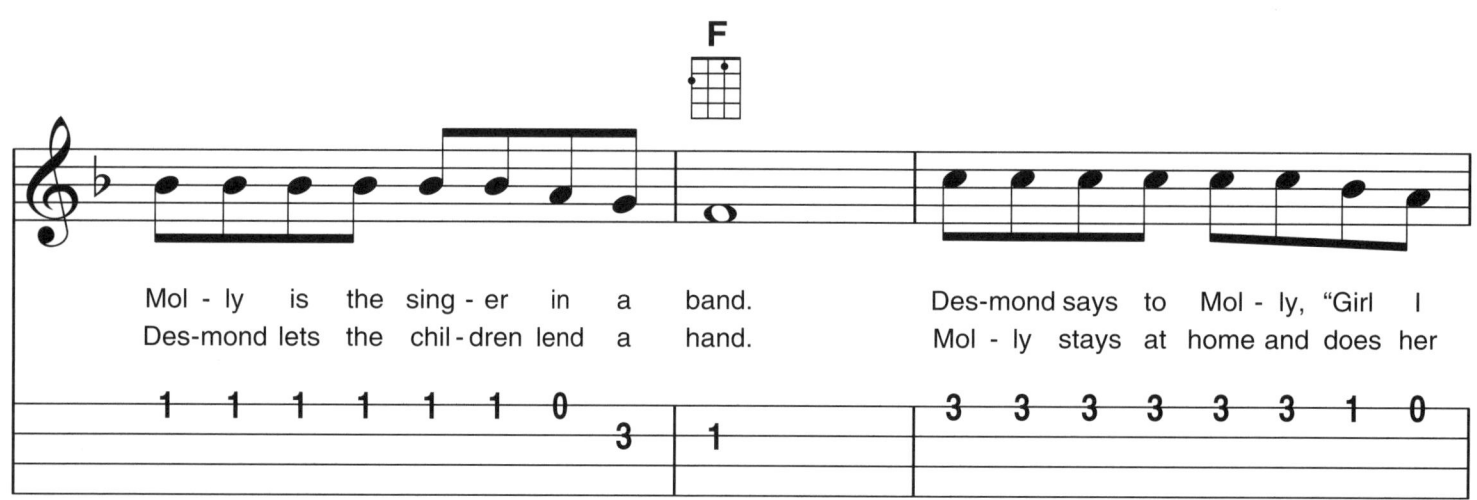

Mol-ly is the sing-er in a band. Des-mond says to Mol-ly, "Girl I
Des-mond lets the chil-dren lend a hand. Mol-ly stays at home and does her

like your face," and Mol-ly says this as she takes him by the
pret-ty face, and in the eve-ning she still sings it with the

Copyright © 1968 Sony/ATV Music Publishing LLC
Copyright Renewed
All Rights Administered by Sony/ATV Music Publishing LLC, 8 Music Square West, Nashville, TN 37203
International Copyright Secured   All Rights Reserved

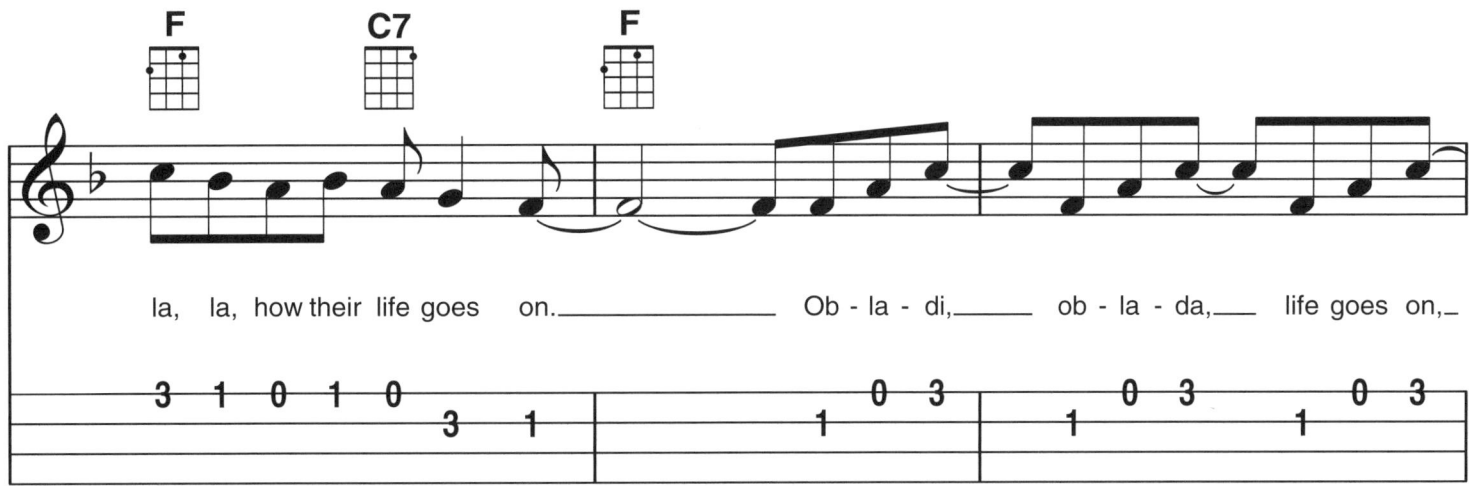
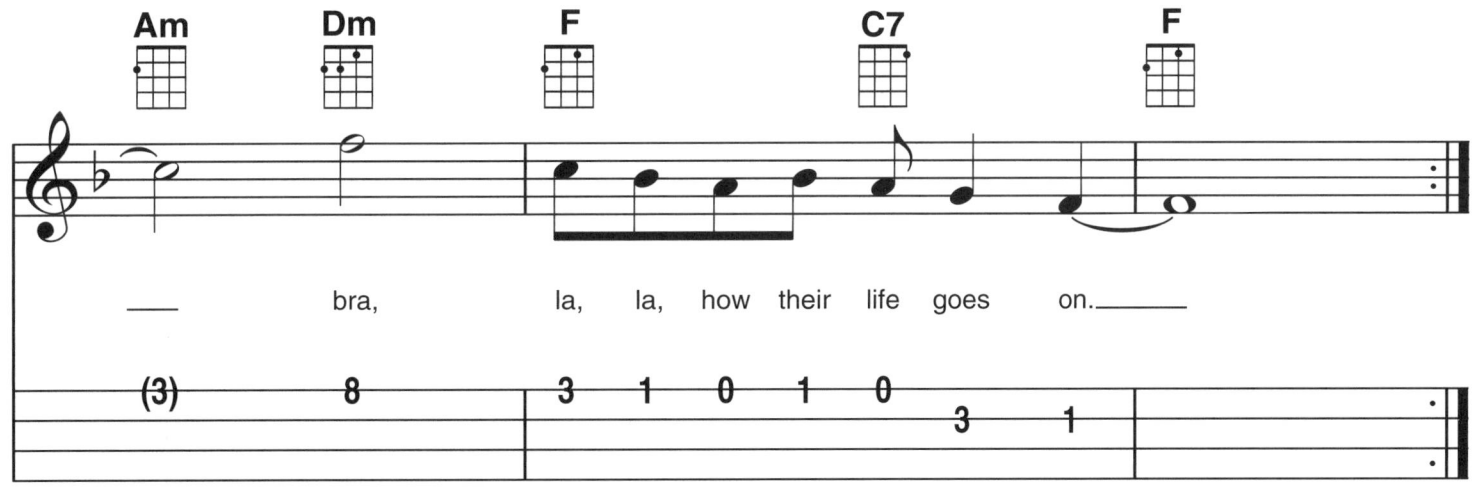

Additional Lyrics

3. Desmond takes a trolley to the jeweler's store,
   Buys a twenty-carat golden ring.
   Takes it back to Molly waiting at the door,
   And as he gives it to her she begins to sing:

4. Happy ever after in the market place,
   Molly lets the children lend a hand.
   Desmond stays at home and does his pretty face,
   And in the evening she's a singer in the band.

Additional Lyrics

2. But now I see,
   What one embrace can do.
   Look at me,
   It's got me loving you.
   Madly;
   That little kiss you stole,
   Held all my heart and soul.

Blue Eyes Crying in the Rain

Words and Music by
FRED ROSE

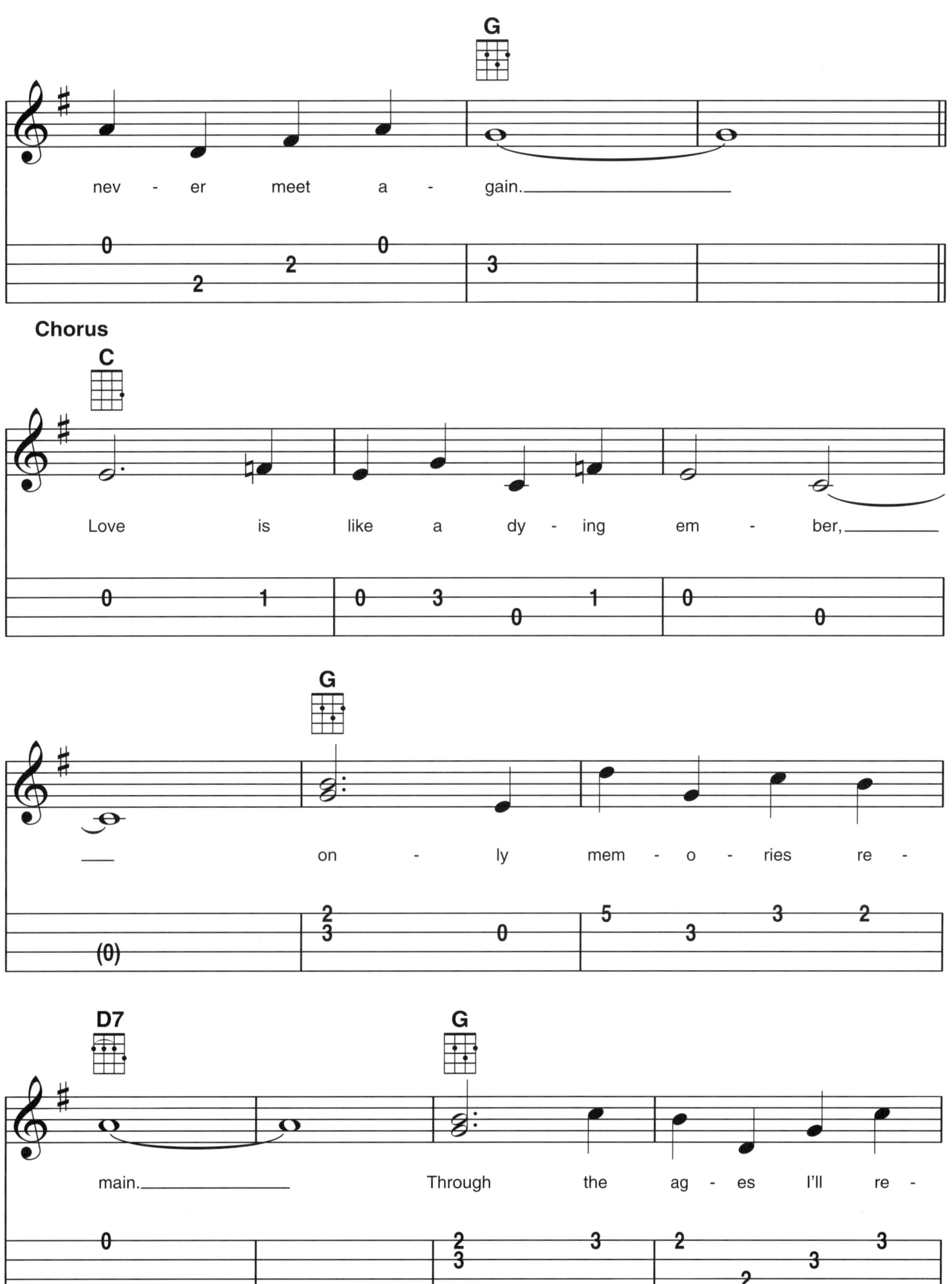

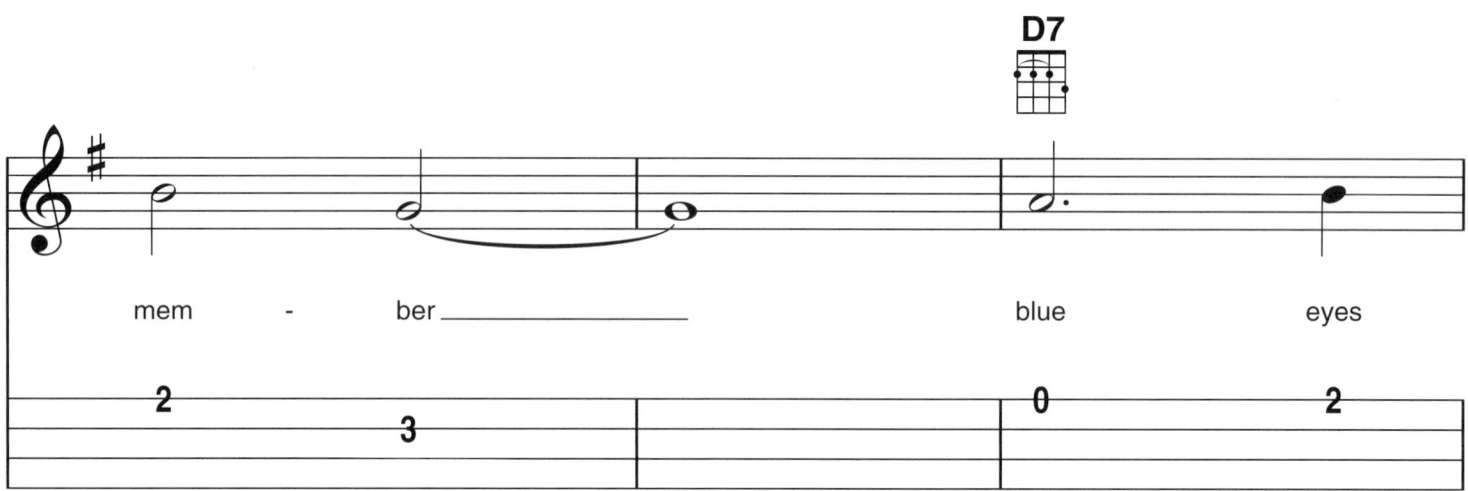

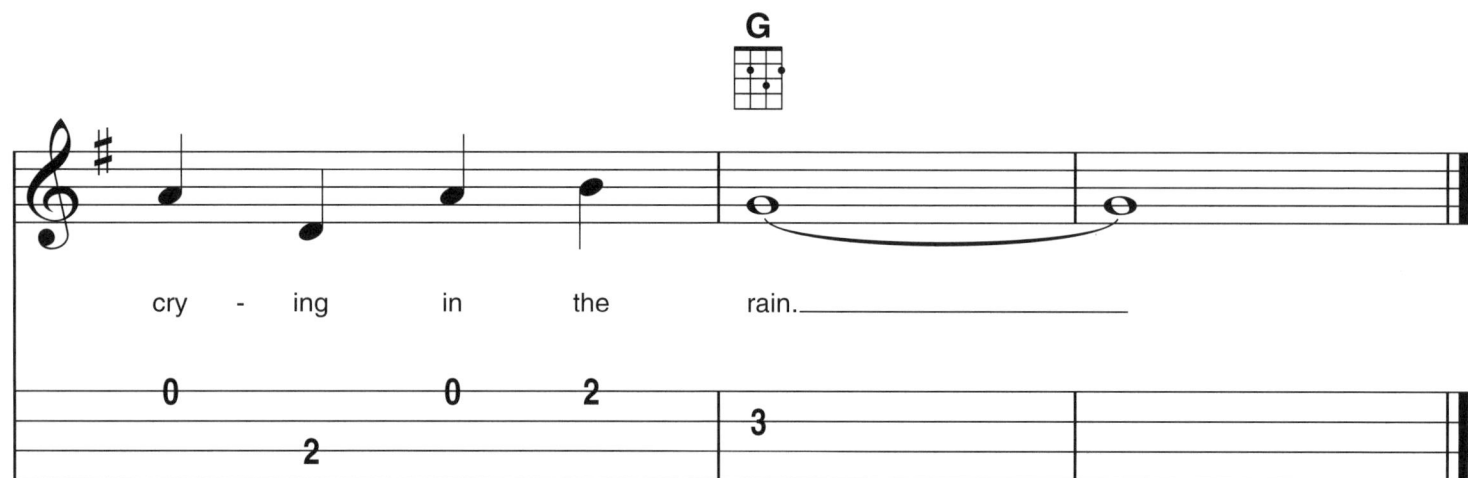

Additional Lyrics

2. Now my hair has turned to silver,
   All my life I've loved in vain.
   I can see her star in heaven,
   Blue eyes crying in the rain.

Chorus: Someday when we meet up yonder,
   We'll stroll hand in hand again.
   In a land that knows no parting,
   Blue eyes crying in the rain.

BLUE SKIES

from BETSY, featured in BLUE SKIES

Words and Music by
IRVING BERLIN

© Copyright 1927 by Irving Berlin
Copyright Renewed
International Copyright Secured   All Rights Reserved

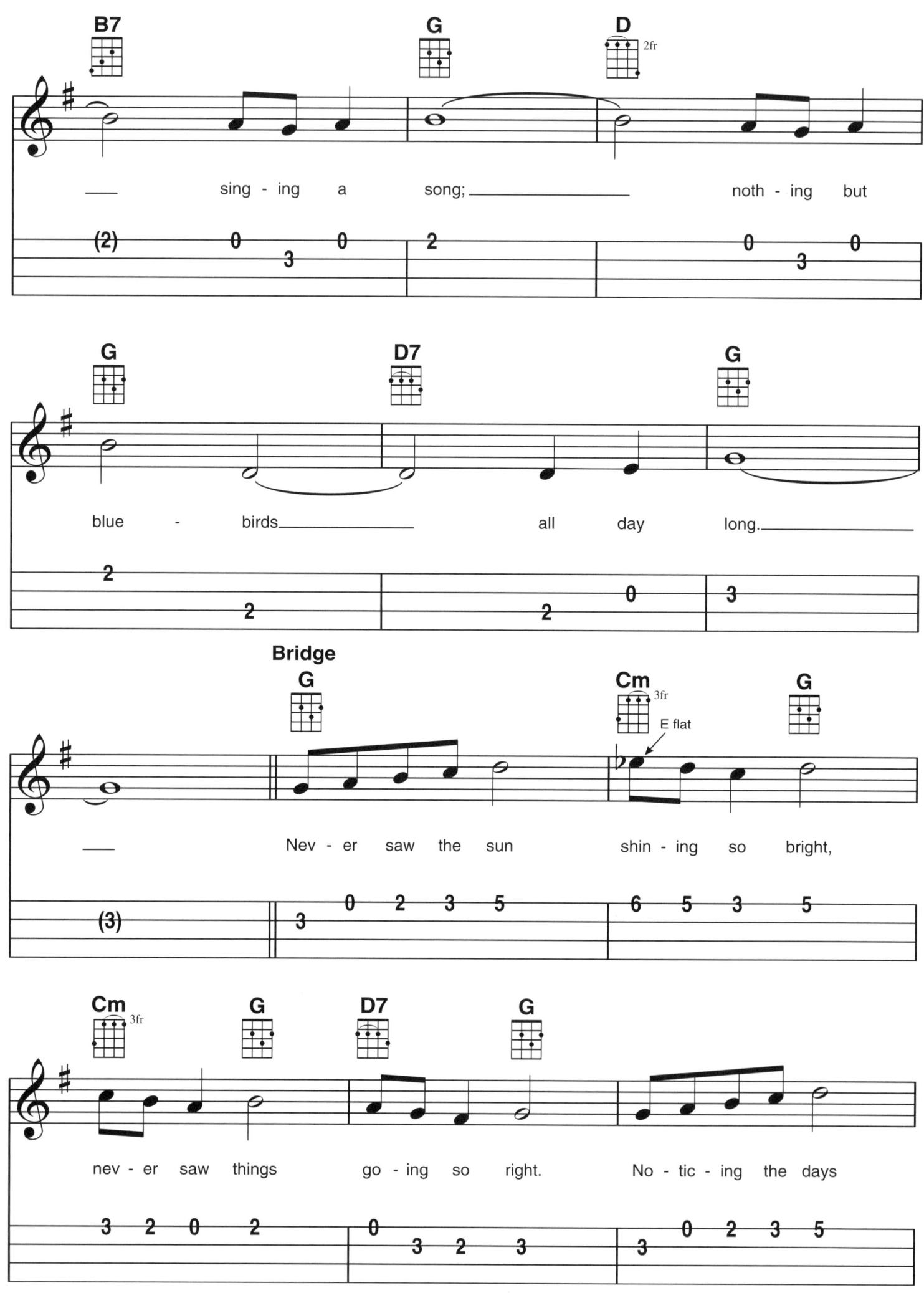

EIGHT DAYS A WEEK

Words and Music by
JOHN LENNON and PAUL McCARTNEY

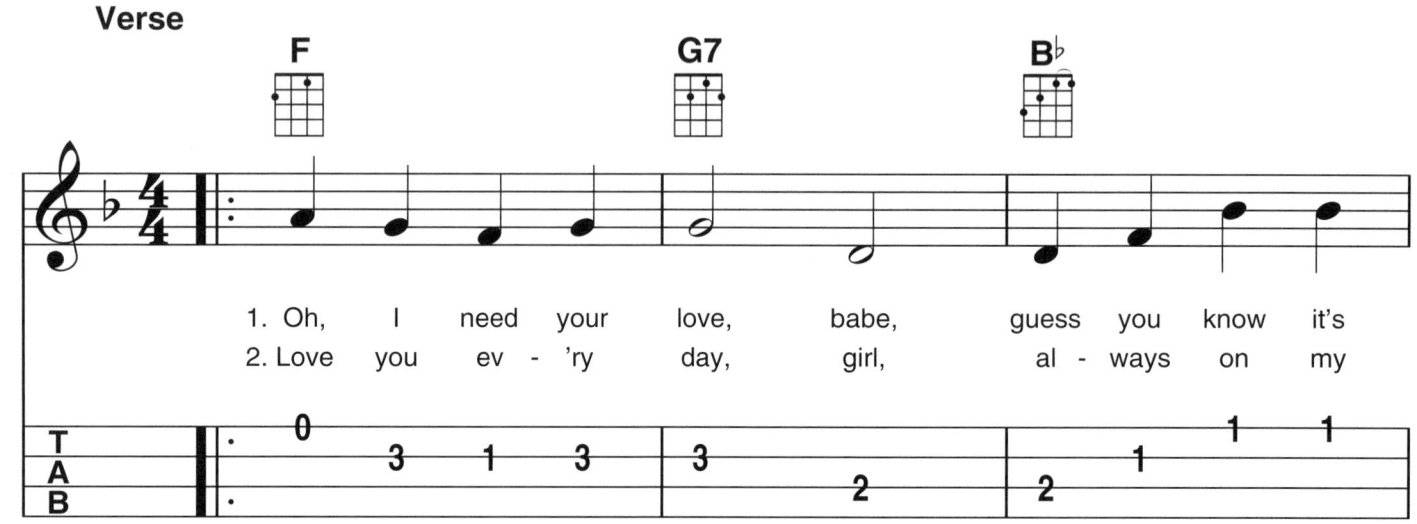

1. Oh, I need your love, babe, guess you know it's
2. Love you ev-'ry day, girl, al-ways on my

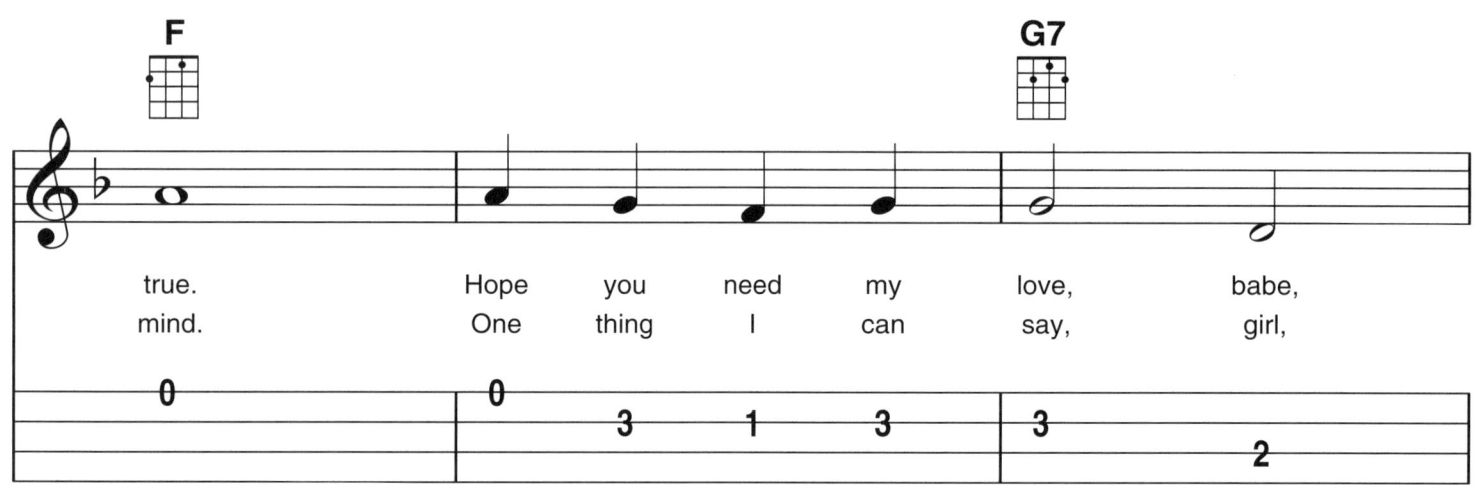

true. Hope you need my love, babe,
mind. One thing I can say, girl,

Chorus

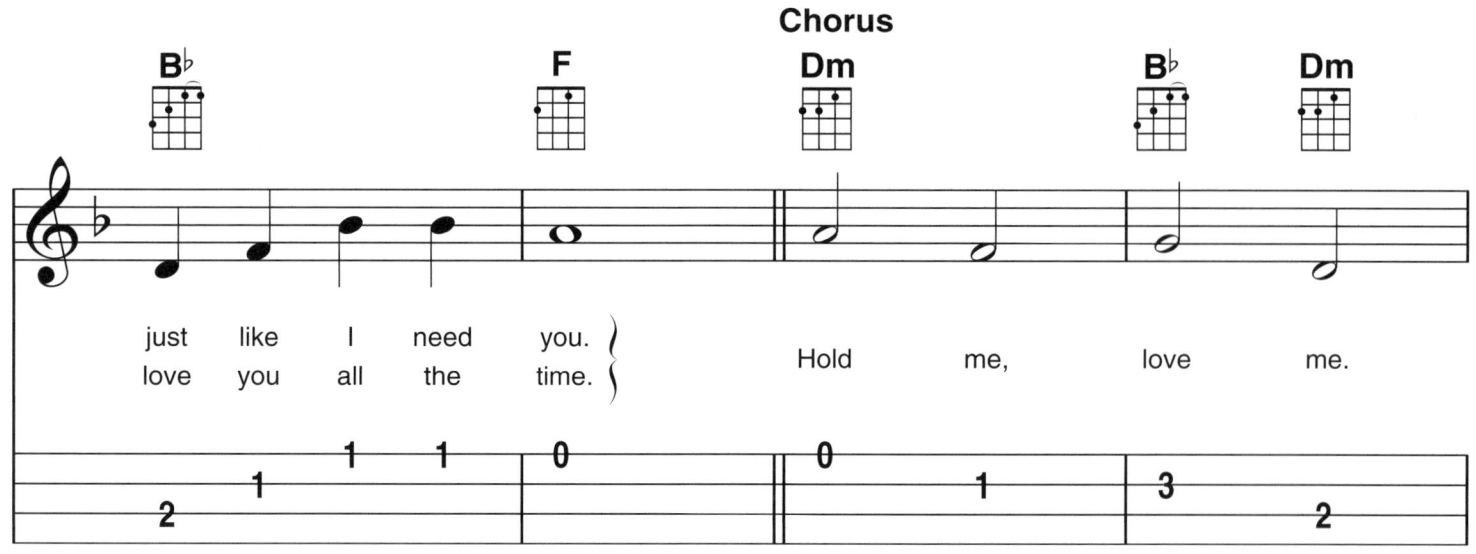

just like I need you.
love you all the time. } Hold me, love me.

Copyright © 1964 Sony/ATV Music Publishing LLC
Copyright Renewed
All Rights Administered by Sony/ATV Music Publishing LLC, 8 Music Square West, Nashville, TN 37203
International Copyright Secured   All Rights Reserved

TOM DOOLEY

**Words and Music Collected, Adapted and Arranged by
FRANK WARNER, JOHN A. LOMAX and ALAN LOMAX
From the singing of FRANK PROFFITT**

Additional Lyrics

3. Trouble, oh, it's trouble, rolling through my breast.
   Long as I'm-a living, boys, ain't-a gonna be no rest.

4. Hand me down my fiddle, play it if you please.
   This time tomorrow, it'll be no use to me.

5. If it weren't for Sheriff Grayson, no trouble would I see.
   If it wasn't for Sheriff Grayson, I'd be in Tennessee.

6. This time tomorrow, where do you reckon I'll be?
   Way down yonder in a hollow, hangin' from a white oak tree.

TRO - © Copyright 1947 (Renewed) and 1958 (Renewed) Ludlow Music, Inc., New York, NY
International Copyright Secured
All Rights Reserved Including Public Performance For Profit
Used by Permission

Blues Stay Away From Me

Words and Music by ALTON DELMORE, RABON DELMORE, WAYNE RANEY and HENRY GLOVER

Additional Lyrics

3. Life is full of misery.
   Dreams are like a memory,
   Bringing back your love that used to be.

4. Tears, so many I can't see.
   Years don't mean a thing to me.
   Time goes by, and still I can't be free.

Copyright © 1949 (Renewed) LOIS PUBLISHING COMPANY
Copyright renewed and controlled in the U.S. by FORT KNOX MUSIC INC., TRIO MUSIC CO., VIDOR PUBLICATIONS, INC.,
UNIVERSAL - SONGS OF POLYGRAM INTERNATIONAL, INC. and LIONEL DELMORE MUSIC CO.
All Rights for LIONEL DELMORE MUSIC CO. and VIDOR PUBLICATIONS, INC. Controlled and
Administered by UNIVERSAL - SONGS OF POLYGRAM INTERNATIONAL, INC.
Copyright controlled outside of the U.S. by FORT KNOX MUSIC INC. and TRIO MUSIC CO.
International Copyright Secured   All Rights Reserved

Learn to play the
Ukulele
with these great Hal Leonard books!

Hal Leonard Ukulele Method Book 1
by Lil' Rev

The *Hal Leonard Ukulele Method* is designed for anyone just learning to play ukulele. This comprehensive and easy-to-use beginner's guide by acclaimed performer and uke master Lil' Rev includes many fun songs of different styles to learn and play. The accompanying CD contains 46 tracks of songs for demonstration and play along. Includes: types of ukuleles, tuning, music reading, melody playing, chords, strumming, scales, tremolo, music notation and tablature, a variety of music styles, ukulele history and much more.

00695847 Book Only $5.95
00695832 Book/CD Pack $9.95
00320534 DVD $14.95

Hal Leonard Ukulele Method Book 2
by Lil' Rev

Book 2 picks up where Book 1 left off, featuring more fun songs and examples to strengthen skills and make practicing more enjoyable. Topics include lessons on chord families, hammer-ons, pull-offs, and slides, 6/8 time, ukulele history, and much more. The accompanying CD contains 51 tracks of songs for demonstration and play along.

00695948 Book Only $5.95
00695949 Book/CD Pack $9.95

Hal Leonard Ukulele Chord Finder
Easy-to-Use Guide to Over 1,000 Ukulele Chords

Learn to play chords on the ukulele with this comprehensive, yet easy-to-use book. *The Ukulele Chord Finder* contains more than a thousand chord diagrams for the most important 28 chord types, including three voicings for each chord. Also includes a lesson on chord construction and a fingerboard chart of the ukulele neck!

00695803 9" x 12" $6.95
00695902 6" x 9" $4.95

Easy Songs for Ukulele
Play the Melodies of 20 Pop, Folk, Country, and Blues Songs
by Lil' Rev

Play along with your favorite tunes from the Beatles, Elvis, Johnny Cash, Woody Guthrie, Simon & Garfunkel, and more! The songs are presented in the order of difficulty, beginning with simple rhythms and melodies and ending with chords and notes up the neck. The audio CD features every song played with guitar accompaniment, so you can hear how each song sounds and then play along when you're ready.

00695904 Book/CD Pack $14.95

Irving Berlin Songs Arranged for the "Uke"

20 great songs with full instructions, including: Alexander's Ragtime Band • White Christmas • Easter Parade • Say It with Music • and more.

00005558 7" x 10-1/4" $6.95

Fretboard Roadmaps – Ukulele
The Essential Patterns That All the Pros Know and Use
by Fred Sokolow & Jim Beloff

Take your uke playing to the next level! Tunes and exercises in standard notation and tab illustrate each technique. Absolute beginners can follow the diagrams and instruction step-by-step, while intermediate and advanced players can use the chapters non-sequentially to increase their understanding of the ukulele. The CD includes 59 demo and play-along tracks.

00695901 Book/CD Pack $14.95

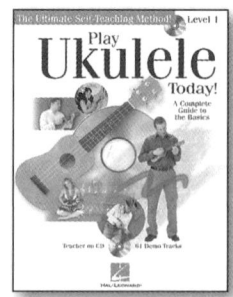

Play Ukulele Today!
A Complete Guide to the Basics
by Barrett Tagliarino

This is the ultimate self-teaching method for ukulele! Includes a CD with full demo tracks and over 60 great songs. You'll learn: care for the instrument; how to produce sound; reading music notation and rhythms; and more.

00699638 Book/CD Pack $9.95

www.halleonard.com

Prices, contents and availability subject to change without notice. Prices listed in U.S. funds.

HAL•LEONARD® CORPORATION
7777 W. BLUEMOUND RD. P.O. BOX 13819
MILWAUKEE, WISCONSIN 53213